Faith of the Butterfly

Susannah Dawn

Faith of the Butterfly

Urano
publishing
Argentina - Chile - Colombia - Spain
USA - Mexico - Peru - Uruguay

Urano
publishing

The first edition of this book was published in January 2024

ISBN: 978-1-953027-30-6

E-ISBN: 978-1-953027-31-3

Printed in Spain

Library of Cataloging-in-Publication Data

Dawn, Susannah

1. Memoir   2. Personal Development

Faith of the Butterfly

Table of Contents

Dedication

*I thank God for opening the doors and placing
the supportive women on my path who always encouraged
and supported me as I began this part of my journey.*

*I am grateful to all the beauty advisors at Sephora who
walked this path with me, always encouraging—yet never
pushing—me to expand my comfort zone, as they became such
an important part of my life.*

*And to my amazing wife and daughters, who supported
me to enter through the doors that opened to me on this
path I've traveled... I love you all.*

Introduction

There are many reasons to forget 2020. Yet for me, it was something positive, a year of significant change. From the age of three, I knew I was female at my core. Unfortunately, due to the era I grew up in and my family background, I quickly learned it was not safe to show my true self in public. My journey through those years was difficult. I was unable to let others know me or my dreams. I feared negative comments or actions from my own family, especially my dad. My body told people I was a boy, and so, I was expected to live like one, play like one—in essence, be strong and rarely show emotions—like a boy. And through it all, it was glaringly obvious to me I was a girl. Unable to live as the girl I knew I was, I moved from being carefree to closing myself off, becoming an introvert for my own safety. The future that had once felt wide open—the one with a multitude of possibilities where I could be and do anything— quickly dwindled when I entered the closet. In the darkness of that small, confined space, I heard my dad and others tell me my interests would lead nowhere; they'd never provide financial success. I had wanted to study astronomy and be a writer, yet those dreams perished in high school as the message of how I had to limit myself to more prosperous niches became ingrained. My dad never saw practical value in my dreams.

At the close of 2019, there was no way to know 2020 would become a year of meaningful transition. A journey, which was halted in so many ways by entering that closet decades ago, was about to start anew and take an unexpected path. It was a period when my evolution from the person others expected me to be based on my shell to living as the woman I've always been at my core, truly began. And being an introvert, the transformation caught me completely off guard. During that time, I changed, grew, and opened to new friends as I began to emerge from the deep, dark closet I'd hid in for so long.

The idea for this memoir came from the realization that I had value, something previously unknown to me. Most of my fifty-plus years were spent on the sidelines and in the shadows, where I remained hidden even though I wanted to participate in life. I had difficulty talking with people. The pressure of what to say to someone after "hi" often wiped my mind blank. I was clueless about conversation protocol. Even basic sentences like, "What do you do?" or "How are you doing?" fled my thoughts.

One reason for this story is to pay tribute to the wonderful associates at "my" Sephora and another cosmetics store in the same mall; they accepted me for the person I was from the very beginning. At this point, it should be noted the names you will see in this memoir are fictitious, yet each one is tied to a real person, often someone who played an important role in my growth during the past two years. Also, I often use the term "my" Sephora store as it was the one place where I always felt at home the moment I stepped through the doors. Many of the beauty advisors there became dear friends. A handful even remember my first months of coming into the store. It was a time when I was afraid to talk with anyone, right before the state shut down for COVID-19. They were welcoming towards me every time I visited, letting me open up to each of them at my own pace. They watched my transformation with their own eyes. As friendships developed, each of the beauty advisors told me how much they saw me grow in both skills and confidence. Their honesty and positive comments were critical in should be to my ability to believe in myself and take each new step out of the closet, into the world. It's from the depths of their love and support that this memoir began.

Therefore, this memoir is my way to review and remember how far I progressed in my transition and growth during such a short, yet extremely important, period of life. It captures the ups and downs as I began to spread my wings like a butterfly for the first time. In a year of significant stay-at-home requirements, there were times when not much really happened. However, towards the end of the summer of 2020, once I started to come out, the speed of my progression from the closet was amazing.

Writing this was also a chance to look at some of the special people who helped me to overcome my fears and move forward on my transformative journey. I counted some of them amongst my few existing friends—individuals who knew me before I started transitioning and accepted me as a trans woman when I came out to them. Just as important were those who were new in my life, the ones who only knew me as Susannah, and became some of my biggest supporters and newest friends.

There is more to my story than what occurred during those short two years of change and reinvention. While I sprinkle in a few actual comments I wrote for Sephora surveys, I also include six personal essays. Each essay is focused on a specific topic of my personal background and was written as a stand-alone story in itself, so let me apologize up front if they seem repetitious. Though I talk about the pain I felt from family and others in these essays, I accept everyone for who they were and are, and I forgive them in my heart, as that is the only way I could begin the true healing process that allowed me to open my wings and fly as my true self. Finally, being a storyteller and writer, there is a short story at the end titled "Hope." It's special to me, as it captures how I've seen my life.

Something that held me back from transition for many years was imposter syndrome: the fear of being pointed out in public for not looking like or being the lady I've always been inside. That fear kept me from going out of the house as my true self for years. Along with that, there was the dysphoria of seeing things about my physical appearance that failed to align with how I really felt and viewed myself as a woman. Even during my early months of transition, when my friends told me they only saw a woman in my photos, it was difficult for me to not see the face I had lived with for so many years. Those issues are also included in these pages, along with some of the ways I overcame them.

Understand that I am one person, one trans woman, and this is my story. Though we're a world of billions, each of us was uniquely created. To me, our uniqueness is part of the second great commandment, "Love your neighbor as yourself." That single statement feels like a cornerstone: guidance to overcome the individual calls to persecute others, to stop criticizing those viewed as different from another's perceived "norm," and to come together in peace.

That brings up another point that was important to me as I began my journey. When the idea of transitioning really manifested itself about five years ago, I actually went to the Bible to search for reasons why I shouldn't—couldn't—transition into the woman I've always been. However, what I found were verses showing me I was exactly who God made me to be, a woman—albeit, a trans woman. Faith and transition went together in my situation; they were not opposed to each other. Thus, I took every significant step—including beginning Hormone Replacement Therapy (HRT) and opening up to strangers who became my closest friends—after much prayer and meditation. It was important to me to remain on the narrow path and pass through the doors God put before me. Those prayers included having and keeping a soft heart, especially when interacting with others. The Lord created me—both how I felt inside, spiritually; and the shell He put me in. Because those two parts of me were often in conflict, it was not until starting and moving through my transition process that peace finally came over me. I grew closer to the Lord as I began to transition into the woman I am today.

Finally, it is important to remember that people don't always stay in one place. By the time I wrote this memoir, many of the friends who were so important to me, so instrumental in my ability to grow into the woman I have become, no longer worked in the stores where they had become such close friends. While they moved on to what I pray are greener pastures, they were essential to my story of growth, and I hope we can remain in contact as I value their friendship. All my life, once someone exited my immediate circle, the relationship was gone. I'm tired of going separate ways and losing connection. My prayer is for that to change and to maintain friendships through the coming years. It is with real friends that life becomes truly blessed and can be lived to its fullest.

Susannah Dawn

1

In the Beginning, There Was... Joy

"I'm not what I used to be, yet I am who I've always been."

—Susannah Dawn

It was the day after Christmas 2019. I was a trans woman who was still buried deep in her closet, which meant the day I walked through the doors of Sephora and stepped into a new world, butterflies fluttered in my stomach. The store was bright, filled with people and their chatter. Daylight entered from both ends of the store: the exterior wall faced an open parking lot, while the mall side had full glass windows and daylight streamed in from the large skylights over the mall hallway. For years I'd wanted to learn more about cosmetics, yet I was held back from visiting any cosmetics stores for fear of what the associates and customers might think. While I could buy cosmetics in the grocery store and then watch online videos about how to apply different types of makeup, I was the type of person who learned much better in hands-on, one-on-one situations.

Thus, on that day, my fears of being outed were strong. True, I had let my dishwater-blonde hair grow for a few years, so it fell just below my shoulders, long enough to at least give me an androgynous appearance. I also wore women's blue jeans and cute sneakers, while my jacket was cinched inside at the waist to create a more feminine appearance to my body. However, I was still sure I'd be spotted for being what I used to be and not who I really was; that someone would point at me, publicly out me, and laugh, telling everyone I was "male." My concerns over what others might think of me and my reasons for being in the store absolutely terrified me.

However, the day after Christmas was also one of the best shopping days of the year to find deals, and it allowed me to spend time with Kim, my middle daughter. Going to Sephora was her idea, yet it gave me a chance to look around the store for myself. While she knew I was a trans woman still hiding in my personal closet, she was also an early supporter. I was always interested in makeup, which she knew; however, my skills were very minimal, and I'd never worn cosmetics of any kind outside the house.

Once in the store, my heart raced as I thought about finding a foundation to practice with at home. I had no expectations to speak with anyone, instead hoping to let my daughter, who knew what I wanted, do all the talking. When one of the ladies came over and asked if we had any questions, Kim took the lead and asked my question. The associate started telling her about foundations and Color Correcting (CC) creams. Their conversation focused on my daughter, though the beauty advisor, whose name I later found out was Joy, often looked at me as if to keep me included in the conversation. It was when I spoke up with a question, though I don't recall what I asked, that Joy dropped her gaze from my daughter and shifted her total focus to me. As she began to explain foundation options to me, Kim quickly headed off to explore the store.

Joy wore thin-rimmed glasses and had blue streaks in her dark hair. I'm six feet tall, and she came up to my shoulders. As I looked at her makeup, it seemed flawless. "What type of look are you going for?" she asked.

"I'd love to be able to do my makeup like you," I said sheepishly, "though for now, I just want to be more androgynous with more neutral tones."

Joy took me around the store to look at different foundations, then offered to color-match one of the brand's samples on my face. I agreed, feeling both nervous and excited. It surprised me that I did not hesitate to let this stranger put makeup on my face in such a spacious, public store.

"Do you have any questions about the foundation?" she asked, sweeping the sample across my cheeks with her brush.

"I'm just beginning," I replied.

"Don't worry about beginning," she said. "It's where you're going that matters, and everyone has to start somewhere." That's when I knew I found someone special in Sephora, a person who truly accepted me, without judgement.

Joy tried a couple of shades on my face, comparing my left and right sides. I listened to every word as she told me what she was doing, how she was putting on the foundation and ways to smooth it out. She had me look in a mirror to see how both products looked, and after seeing the difference between each side, we agreed on which I liked best.

"Here's a towel if you'd like to wipe everything off," she said, "or I can just clean off your left side and finish it with the foundation you like."

I had a brief pause as I contemplated what she had said. Then, to my surprise, I asked her to do my whole face.

Joy had a way of keeping my attention focused on her, as if she could sense my fear of looking around the store and potentially seeing other people staring at me. I felt safe talking with her. As she finished applying the foundation, I pondered how easy it was for me to accept her suggestions. Joy offered to put a sample together that would allow me to try the product at home for a couple of days. Since she had to go on break, she asked another associate to help. That beauty advisor was also kind, though I sensed she may not have been as right a person to help me from the start as Joy was; I'm not sure I could have opened up to her in the same way.

Even with all the people around me in the store, there was a sense of something special going on inside of me. For the first time in my life, I was starting to let strangers in, while giving the real me a chance to step out. The butterflies still fluttered, and the fears still tried to take control of my actions. However, on that day I was starting to feel... right.

After going around the store with Kim, I headed towards the entrance when I saw Joy was back. I could barely contain a smile and my joy as she beamed and came over to me. "Do you have any other questions?"

"I'm curious about foundation for eye shadow. I noticed some of those products while we were browsing."

She took me over to one of the brand areas saying, "This is my favorite foundation for eyeshadow." Placing a small amount on the back of my hand, she had me rub it in to get a feel for it. "As you can see, you only need a little for each use."

My next question seemed a natural progression of our conversation, "What color eyeshadows would be best for me?"

"Almost any color would look good on you, and there's a new product that just came out today. If you see a palette you like, I can put it on you." While looking over the different shades, I had difficulty choosing just one of the color palettes. Joy picked up an eyeshadow palette labeled "Rose."

That was my introduction to Fenty! Joy took me to a mirror where I could watch as she applied many different shades of red across my left eyelid. There were six shades to choose from; Joy used four. She verbalized step-by-step instructions of what she was doing, letting me know why she put certain shades along different parts of my eyelids. When she finished, she asked, "Is there another shade you'd like to try?"

Soon she was doing my right eye with a neutral palette.

After I compared how each looked on me, Joy said, "I can remove the eyeshadows if you want, or make both lids match."

"Can we just remove the left side and match it with my right?" The words came that easy to me. Not only was I wearing foundation, now there would be a beautiful, soft, neutral shade of eyeshadow on my lids. It still felt surreal to actually wear makeup in public, even if it was only in the store.

When Joy returned with a cloth to remove the rose shadow, a second lady came over with her. "She asked to try the eye shadow, and this palette looks good on her," Joy told the second associate, who agreed.

A nervous excitement swept over me at her words when I realized what Joy said. It was the first time anyone had referred to me as "she" in public, and a slight anxiety fluttered in my stomach as I was unsure how I looked to the other person. The anxiety was quickly doused by the joy of hearing those words uttered by strangers; it was a euphoric thrill to feel accepted by both ladies. The biggest surprise came when it dawned on me that I had almost missed the reference, Joy said it so naturally.

Once done, I asked about an eyeshadow brush. Leading me to a selection of makeup brushes, Joy said, "This would be a good first brush." She then gave me a new product to add to my basket.

Supported by a wonderful beauty advisor, there I was, wearing foundation and eyeshadow in public for the first time. A plethora of emotions flowed through me. I was excited and happy that an associate could be so kind and gentle with me during that first shopping experience, helping me to learn about makeup and find products to work with at home. At the same time, I was worried someone might look at me and make a derogatory comment. However, Joy's friendly nature allowed me to remain focused on her as we continued to talk.

"Do you have any other questions?" she asked.

"I'm not sure about blush."

To be honest, I had no idea where that question came from. Maybe it popped up because Joy made it easy to ask her anything about makeup. Her eyes seemed large behind her glasses, somehow keeping mine focused on her. She never stopped smiling as she assisted me, and between her calm eyes and smile, I felt safe.

Walking to a small selection of blushes, Joy said, "This is my favorite blush." She picked up a soft, light-pink shade.

After putting some on a blush brush, she showed me how to put it on. She started by my left ear and swooped the brush towards the corner of my mouth, then kept swirling it in the cheek area above that line. "Although the powder's gone from the brush, the continual swooshing helps to even it out on your cheek." As I looked at the result in the mirror she said, "Would you like me to do the other side?"

"Yes," I said without hesitation.

It was while she put blush on me that I asked her name. I wasn't used to talking with strangers, much less asking their name, but with her, I felt safe. "Joy," she said.

I knew God put Joy in Sephora that day just for me. Her patience and delightful personality were amazing. I was afraid to tell anyone about being transgender. To be transparent about that with someone, especially someone I just met, required them to calmly and figuratively put their arms around me with love and care. They needed to answer my questions without ever implying that what I was doing was wrong. That was Joy. She was the right lady to help guide me on my first steps of learning the art of makeup so I could begin to let my true, feminine self out. I often looked into her brown eyes as she spoke of the techniques she was using. That simple act confirmed I trusted her; if I'm unable to look someone in the eyes, then it's likely there's something about them I don't quite trust.

After paying for my purchases, I thanked Joy for her help as I headed for the exit. Passing through the doors while wearing makeup in public was like passing into a new era. My emotions were mixed. There was excitement as it felt good to take those initial steps to finally come out as the woman I always knew I was. There was also fear of being spotted and ridiculed as it was my first time wearing makeup in public. It helped to have my daughter with me. As we began to walk through the mall, I slowly felt more at ease with my new look.

As we continued shopping, we entered different stores, and each time, I found myself to still be a little self-conscious about wearing makeup in public. Eventually, the fears began to dissipate until they were no longer a constant at the forefront of my thoughts. I began to feel a little more confident in myself with makeup on. Just a small amount of neutral-toned cosmetics allowed me to feel more true to my inner self, and was part of the reason I was comfortable making a purchase at the next cosmetics store we visited.

It was a MAC store attached to Macy's. Kim's focus was on the lipsticks. I also took the opportunity to look at the different shades, considering what might align with my natural lip color. Between my makeup and long hair, I felt more at ease to consider wearing a neutral lipstick in public. And yet, there was still a little dread that someone I knew might see me shopping. The entire side of the store was open to the mall, allowing anyone in the area to easily see me looking at the different cosmetics. There was a change in sales ladies. Linda, who was as tall as me, though much thinner, took over. Her dark hair fell to her shoulders. What struck me were her really cute silver-rimmed glasses. Like Joy, Linda was wonderful. She helped me find a shade I felt I could wear without anyone noticing I was wearing lipstick. Our shopping trip occurred before COVID, meaning Linda could let me test the colors on my lips.

The MAC store was exposed to the rest of the mall, so I was more nervous trying on lipstick than I had been in the more enclosed Sephora store. At the same time, I felt invigorated to be doing this so publicly. When Kim found a lipstick and lipliner combo that was on sale, each of us bought one. I also bought a lipstick shade that aligned with my natural lip color and put it on before we left the store. Amazingly, I found myself walking around the mall wearing foundation, eye shadow, blush, and lipstick.

My coming-out process officially started. I interacted with sales ladies as a woman for the first time, and they were fully accepting of me. Although I didn't know it at the time, my transition to Susannah had begun.

2

A Short Bit-o-Background

In my early years I was a carefree child with no concept of limitations to what I could do. The world was an open book for me to be me—to draw and color whatever I wanted. It was easy to play with other children, run around, and have fun no matter where I was at the time. Decades after my aunt's wedding, she often reminded me adults had to hold me still for photos by placing their hands on my shoulders because I wouldn't stop moving, and in those days, it was hard to take a good picture if people didn't stay still. Her words were another reminder of how carefree I was before I retreated into my own closet around age seven.

As early as three, I knew I was a girl, not a boy. This was not a "feeling" or "identification." It was truth. At that young age, my nightly prayer to God was to wake up as a girl. By age seven, I began to exhibit my inner girl, to my dad's chagrin. If I was caught in my mother's clothes, I was spanked. If I acted in a manner he deemed girlish, I was ridiculed and teased. I'm sure if I had been vulnerable and told my dad the truth, he'd have responded harshly that I was a boy, and that's how I should act. It seemed my dad did everything he could to squash every ounce of girl in me, to force me to grow up as a boy—as his oldest son. I'm sure he believed his tactics were proper and successful. However, he never knew the truth of his tactics, never understood how his actions pushed me away from him and left me unable to feel safe around men.

It was because I felt restrained, forced to be someone who wasn't the real me, that I withdrew from my family, friends, and the world. I became an introvert who knew in her heart she was a girl yet had to pretend to be something else. That truth had to remain hidden so no one could ridicule her. It became safer for me to say as little to my parents as possible. My dad's rejection of my true self was fresh in my early years, leaving wounds that would take decades to heal. In my heart, even though I knew he loved me, I also understood that I had to limit my trust in him. His teasing and ridicule were intolerable, so it was safest to say nothing.

By the time I entered middle school, I had no friends. There was no one to hang out with on the playground or in my classes. Playing with the other boys was out, as I knew they didn't like me. That sentiment had been demonstrated repeatedly, including when I defeated a popular boy in wrestling. Most of the students cheered for him, and no one congratulated me for my win. Then there was the boy who bullied me throughout middle school. I never told anyone about him, as I didn't expect to receive any support. Instead, I tried to always keep as far away as possible from my bully.

My self-esteem entering middle school was already low. The more I hid myself, the more I remained alone, and the lower it got. By high school, even though we moved cross country to a new city and a chance to start over, I never felt important to anyone. It was still difficult to make friends, and I didn't trust my parents enough to let them know how alone I felt. Though I put on a good face in public, all it really did was provide a nice frosting to cover the ugly pain inside. I felt depressed, rejected, and alone. I couldn't see signs of anyone liking me because I kept withdrawing further into the darkness of my closet.

The understanding that I was a girl at heart—at my core—never left me. I didn't "feel" or "identify" as a girl; I was a girl. It pained me to know I couldn't share that joyous side of myself with anyone, and I could only let her out if I was alone. It wasn't fulfilling because I was only being honest with myself within a closet that hid me from the rest of the world. I wanted to live my life in the open, to enjoy myself and go everywhere as a girl. Having to hide away was like living in purgatory rather than having the full life we all deserve.

After high school, I tried my best to live as a man. In college I joined the military through ROTC and graduated with my degree and a commission as an Army officer. For over a dozen years, as a National Guard cavalry officer, I hid my true identity. At the same time, I joined my dad's company, where I worked for almost twenty years. I started there when he told me I had to find a job, or work for him. As I had no idea what I was qualified to do, the easy route was to work for him. It could have been a place to try to heal the rift with my dad and create a more trusting relationship; instead, the rift only widened. If I asked him a question that could have brought new opportunities to the firm, his standard response was, "Why?" I felt unseen and unheard, so it was another place where I had to keep my true nature hidden. I wasn't strong enough to pull myself out of the company until I went back to school for a business degree.

I was also married... twice. Both times, the women knew I cross-dressed before we married, and still they said they loved me. It turned out that my first wife only tolerated my feminine self. Over time, she refused to accept or tolerate that part of me. She filed for divorce, complaining I wasn't the same person she'd married. It was as though I was not allowed to grow over time, that I should have stagnated and remained the same person I'd been almost two decades earlier. She had a counselling background, so when I exhibited anything she didn't like, there were usually two options. First, I went to a counselor to get "fixed," yet he said I was fine. Second, we ended up in couples counseling, which seemed to fix whatever the problem was for about six months before she said we needed to go back. In the latter years of the marriage, we adopted an infant daughter. My ex knew I always wanted a daughter, and possibly thought adding a little girl to our family would stabilize us, as I loved my daughter and wanted to spend all the time I could with her. During the divorce process, everyone asked me to talk with them, to let them know how I was feeling. Having been so withdrawn most of my life, it was difficult. I tried it once, and quickly learned it was not wise to let any family members know about my life or how I felt. Anything I said was filtered by the third party with whom I spoke, then passed back to my soon-to-be ex, as happened when I opened up to her mom on a trip we took alone to the store. Whether her mom was trying to help didn't matter. Everything I said was relayed to my ex, who spent three hours grilling me on the conversation. I understood, then, that most family members aligned with my ex and were more supportive of her than of me. I learned there was no one I could trust.

In my second marriage, I finally found someone who understood that each of us needed to grow, and it was best to grow together. She accepted all of me. As I became more and more vulnerable about my feminine identity, she was there, loving and supporting me. She was the first person to encourage me to go out wearing whatever I felt comfortable wearing, even if it was a skirt or dress. I deeply appreciated the support, and though I wasn't ready to take such steps publicly, it was affirming to be able to be myself at home without having to hide.

Due to COVID and work, we've been apart for well over a year. However, we are constantly in touch with each other, and I've kept her updated with photos showing me finally being my womanly self. She's seen how I look when I go out, and her support has been amazing! She often tells me that she sees how beautiful, happy, and confident I am in the pictures. On my birthday, during the first part of 2021, she even texted, "You are sparkling," and "You are a new born lady ~ a brand new life!" I couldn't ask for a more supportive person in my world.

3

Christmas 2019

At the end of 2019, my transition to Susannah was underway. In Joy, I found someone who was accepting and very helpful. Before meeting her, I was scared, even terrified, that my steps towards being Susannah while out in the world would be snuffed out through ridicule, implying I was an imposter. It was important to have support from my wife and three daughters. However, it wouldn't be until sometime in 2021 that I considered telling my parents, siblings, or any other blood relative.

Over the previous three years, I had varying conversations about my true self with my wife and two youngest daughters. Starting in April 2017, I let my hair grow. By Christmas 2019, I'd had no haircuts except a Christmas-Eve trim. Just before Thanksgiving that same year, I pierced my ears for the first time. It was something I'd wanted to do for a long time yet had denied for fear of what my dad and others might say. My confidence was low when dealing with others, yet I'd always wanted to wear earrings, especially those that dangled. My confidence was growing.

On Christmas, the day before meeting Joy, I came out to my oldest daughter Lauren and her wife Allison. Although Kim was there, I hoped she would keep quiet as making the announcement was something I needed to do without assistance. I rarely saw my oldest daughter due to how far away she lived. We weren't exactly close, as I didn't enter her life until

she was well into high school, and at that time, she still lived with her father. On that Christmas day, however, the distance between us began to
close when, after exchanging gifts, I told her I was trans. The relief I felt
saying the words was almost overshadowed by an anticlimactic feeling as
Lauren and Allison just looked at me in a way that felt like they already
knew, or they were being polite to not overwhelm me with questions. No
matter the reason, their support and love were unmistakable.

That day began a bond with them that I hadn't expected. It was slow
to develop, yet I felt safe with them in a way I hadn't felt around people
in a long time. It took about six months of intermittent contact before I
began to really open up. From there, I felt a closeness with them; they
were my kids, and as such, supported me as I've always seen myself. They
only gave me positive encouragement.

In June, I began to update them on my writing projects as well as express my concerns when COVID cases were on the rise in their area. I sent
them website updates and some of the stories I was writing. I ran my pen
name, "Susannah Dawn," past them before submitting my first story to
the Writers of the Future contest. Set in the future, the story follows a
cavalry officer who transitions during her service to become the first trans
woman given a combat-unit command. It chronicles some of the issues
she had to deal with before and during her first combat action. My story
received an honorable mention, and it felt validating to have my first submission as Susannah Dawn receive such recognition.

The first time leaving the house as Susannah was a few days after Christmas when Kim and I went to ZooLights. Although dark outside, I was still
nervous about what people might think when they saw me. My outfit included skinny jeans, tall brown boots, a tan turtleneck sweater, green
jacket, and a purse. Driving to the zoo was the easy part. Once out of the
car, I became apprehensive of everyone around me. To allay my nerves, I
kept my attention on Kim as we walked and talked. The weather was nice
for that time of year, not wet or cold, so the walk through the parking lot
felt good. However, showing my driver's license to the gate attendant to
enter the zoo was more nerve-racking. The way I appeared in front of the

lady checking my ID was nothing like my photo—starting with the length of my hair. Fortunately, she just smiled and let us pass to enter the zoo.

It became an evening of many firsts, including the first time I had photos taken as Susannah outside the house. Kim was always big on pictures, especially selfies. She took the first-ever pictures of me in public. What a mix of emotions I had as I stood near that large lawn area! There was the thrill of having my photo—as Susannah—out in the world, and the worry that someone might say something out of place as I stood alone by the lawn with nowhere to hide. Walking towards the exit, she shot more photos in the colorfully lit tunnel area. Part of me felt a need to do those pictures as quickly as possible so people wouldn't be able to really look at me under the colored lights. I also wanted to take my time, enjoy the moment, and get the best shots possible. They were the first photos to proclaim that I was finally stepping out into the world as myself.

Looking back on those early transition photos, it's important I step back and acknowledge them for what they really are: photos of a lady just starting to find her way in the world. They may not show the most beautiful woman; I see my old face in them, yet what matters is how they provide an image of where I started. That allows me to see my own progression from what I was in the past, to now, when I am finally beginning to match who I've always been. They are a reminder of where I was when I finally began to put myself out in the world, to risk fear and ridicule while seeking support.

I understand how many people in this country view the transgender community in negative ways. Often, they point to aspects of the Bible to express their views. At other times, their weapon of choice is science. However, they fail to consider—or even understand—that one can walk with God and still be transgender. God looks at the heart and is always beside us on the paths He specifically made for each of us.

For me, every day of this journey included talking with God, looking to Jesus, and making sure I remained on the path that He made for me to walk. I needed God's input, His affirmation, His opening of doors regarding my transition to become as female on the outside as I was on the inside. There were times when I felt this direction, this path in life, had been put on my heart for His glory.

I believe each person's relationship with their creator is unique. That's an important aspect of who I am. It's why, when I pray, I often ask about His will and what He placed me here to accomplish. Often there's no firm, attributable answer. However, at the end of December 2019, He showed me specific examples to answer my questions.

The first included a Sunday in November after I pierced my ears. I went to church, though it was a difficult decision to go that day, as I feared being judged for having small stud earrings. I sat near the back, keeping to myself at the end of the pew only a couple rows from the doors.

During the greeting time, I remained seated, as was my habit. A woman walking up the aisle to the back of the sanctuary caught my eye. As she was about to pass me, she placed her hand on my left shoulder and said, "Glad you are here." Before the service started, an elderly lady at the other end of my pew got up and walked over to welcome me to church. Then the lady who sat to my right spoke with me a couple of times in nice tones. I was greeted with grace by three separate women.

God often reminded me how He brought me and my wife together, creating a feeling of safety. After telling her my deepest secret, that I was a cross-dresser, her response was, "I already knew that." She calmly let me know how she already perceived my female "interior." She knew before I asked her to marry me, and she still loved me. From there, it became obvious how loving and accepting my family was, supporting me to be my true self even if it were to include transitioning to female. Five special women in my family love me, and it's not because they are related by blood. Instead, we are related by the love in our hearts that brought us together.

Then, I was reminded of the trip to the mall the day after Christmas. One of the first stores Kim and I entered was Alter'd State. Once inside, we were greeted with, "Hello Ladies." Kim looked at me with a knowing smile. I felt warm in my heart. It felt so right to be accepted as a lady. Then there was Sephora, where Joy helped me with foundation and other cosmetic questions. Her supportive nature, how she always called me "she" and "her" when speaking about me with other sales ladies, was what truly helped me begin to overcome the fears that kept me hidden away.

2019 ended in a way that I never imagined. For a half century, taking even small steps towards my true self felt unimaginable. Yet the last six weeks of the year saw seismic shifts in my life: pierced ears, allowing makeup to be put on me in Sephora (and keeping it on when I left the store), and going out to the zoo as a woman.

Making such strides at the end of the year felt like a miracle. I began to wonder what was in store for 2020.

4

January Starts a Very Different Year

Entering 2020, I wasn't sure how I would let go of the last residues of what I was, to let my womanhood thrive. Looking back, I see New Year's Day provided a glimpse that foreshadowed my year. Kim and I returned to Sephora. It was a day that turned out to be almost as special as meeting Joy. Kim had some foundation questions that she asked the sales associate. The associate was about a half-foot shorter than me with dark hair and eyes, and a charming smile. When she mentioned having oily skin, I began to ask her questions about products, and ultimately, her name.

"Catherine," she said. "What's your name?"

I slowly responded with my male name. However, there was a distinct and unspoken question in her eyes: *"Is that your final answer?"* It was as though she was verifying whether I wanted to stick with my answer or reconsider my words to provide what she knew was the more correct response.

"Susannah," I said.

Catherine then asked, "Which do you prefer?"

I stumbled. Things were moving so fast all I could tell her was that I wasn't quite sure and seemed to be bouncing between the two. I felt fortunate that Catherine said nothing about my response. Her patience reminded me of Joy.

Catherine's focus was on skincare, a new topic for me. She emphasized the importance of daily skincare routines. She then took a strip of register tape and wrote down a beginner's routine for both morning and evening to make sure I followed a plan designed to improve my skin. I greatly appreciated her taking the time to write the schedule down, which I followed as best I could with the products I had.

The following week I went to Sephora on my own, and Joy was there. She was busy with a customer, but when our eyes met, her face lit up. It was the first time I can remember anyone having that reaction towards me. When she was free to help me, it seemed like she wanted to give me a hug. She touched my arm lightly, like a friend. Then she made my day saying, "Your makeup looks great!"

Wow! I was worried about how I looked in public, as makeup was such a new aspect of my life. Her feedback told me I was on the right path.

I felt calm and true to myself around Joy. When she noticed I was looking at photos on my phone, she asked to see them. "It would be good to photograph your journey," she said. Joy felt like the big sister I'd been missing all my life.

That same day, Joy asked my name.

"Susannah," I replied, for the first time not stuttering between two names.

"That's what I wanted," she said.

After getting lunch in the food court, I returned home. Once there, I realized I'd been going out as a trans woman for almost two weeks. While my outfits were nothing exceptional: just sneakers, jeans, and sweaters, they were also made complete by the makeup I wore. Although my appearance might still be viewed as androgynous, no one looked at me strangely when I walked through the mall. I felt comfortable that everyone accepted me.

The next week I took what felt like a huge risk. I went to the mall wearing skinny jeans and knee-high boots. It was the same outfit as my night at the zoo. My hope was to see Joy in Sephora. I was curious of how she'd react. Unfortunately, she wasn't in that day. I spoke with Brenda, someone I'd seen in the store during my previous visits. Standing about the same height as Catherine, with bright-blue eyes and dark hair, she kindly answered my questions. No one said anything about my outfit, and while my visit to Sephora had some positive aspects, my confidence waned without Joy's friendly face in the store. Joy was supportive of my expanding boundaries as I tried to slowly, safely, navigate the steps and risks of coming out as a woman. I was gripped by the need to leave the mall and made a hasty retreat to the sanctuary of my car. I had a strong urge to go home where it was safe. I knew I'd taken a major step by wearing the outfit, yet it didn't feel entirely rewarding. In many ways, it was essential to have a crutch, something or someone I could turn to for support.

It was a time of uncertainty on my journey. I took baby steps towards presenting as the woman I'd always known I was inside. Simultaneously, it was the period most likely to send me running back into my closet. That was a strong possibility, especially being alone all the time as I had no friends to hang out with, and my wife and daughters all lived at least a thousand miles away. Even though I felt safe about my appearance, when I walked through the mall, ate in the food court, or went to the grocery store, part of me was waiting for negative comments to prove I was an imposter, to tell me I didn't belong in this world as the woman I was created to be. My fears were rooted in experiences I'd had with my dad and were compounded by anti-trans comments I saw on social media. I leaned on faith that I'd be alright walking outside as myself, as Susannah. To my relief, I never noticed quizzical looks, heard derogatory comments, or felt threatened. I knew my relief came from the Lord, whether He blocked them from me, or kept hearts soft around me.

It was the end of January when my confidence received a needed boost from an unexpected source. By that time, I recognized two sales ladies in MAC: Linda, who helped me with my first lipstick, and a second lady who looked similar to Linda. Something about the second lady encouraged me to talk with her. I wondered if maybe she was also a trans woman. I didn't know anyone in the trans community, so I hoped meeting someone would have a positive impact on me and my growth. My problem was how to talk with her. Sure, it was a makeup store, and I could ask questions about the products. However, being an introvert made it difficult.

I entered the store and both ladies were there. It seemed like the second one might have recognized me as I made a beeline to talk with her.

My words stumbled a bit as we began to talk. It was more difficult than I expected to tell her I was looking for a new lipstick with a bit more color than the shades I already had. We walked to the lipstick section to begin looking at colors.

"I'm new to wearing makeup," I said.

"That's alright," she replied, "I've only been wearing makeup for four years." She confirmed she was also a trans woman, and I was excited to meet someone with whom I could chat.

"I just started after Christmas," I said, "after over fifty years of not really doing anything."

"Wow!" she said. "You've only been doing this for a month and you're doing a great job with your eyebrows. That's something many women have problems with right now."

She asked if I wanted to go over to the big mirrors to try the lipsticks, and I agreed. That's when she told me her name was Josie.

"What's your name?" she asked.

"It'll say (legal name) in the computer," I said.

"What's your true name?"

"Susannah," I said, "although my daughter likes to call me Suzie."

Josie was almost as tall as me. Her hair was long with soft curls, much darker than mine, and some light highlights at the ends. She told me she was of Hispanic heritage, and when her brown eyes caught my attention, I was in awe of how well she did her eye shadow. I also thought her voice was beautiful. She wore a gorgeous black dress with lace at the neck and sleeves.

"I feel like I'm still hiding a bit wearing my jeans and sneakers, though last week I wore skinny jeans and boots."

"Brown boots," she said. "I saw you last week."

Although I didn't say anything, her observation caught me by surprise. On that trip, I only went as far as Sephora in the mall, so I wasn't quite sure how she could have seen me. However, I did tend to walk through the mall with my blinders on to avoid eye contact and the possibility of being outed. Even in Sephora, I kept them on, looking for Joy or any other familiar face as opposed to talking with anyone new. Blinders provided a sense of safety in public.

Josie put two different lipsticks on me. Both were brighter and more purply-red than my usual colors. I liked "Amorous" the best, and when she did the Amorous with lip liner on me, it looked beautiful!

"Do you want to go out with that one, or go back to the Laissez-Faire you had on?" she asked.

I went back to the more neutral color in my purse. Josie cleaned off the Amorous lipstick, powdered around my lips to replace the makeup that was removed, then lined my lips before I put on my lipstick.

Josie gave me her business card with color swatches of the other lipstick and liner I liked. On the other side, she wrote her social media link for me.

Is it alright to change your name in the computer, Susannah?" she asked at the register.

"Yes," I said. Both her question and my quick response surprised me. It was becoming easier to be myself publicly.

After putting the lipstick in my purse, I turned to leave the store. Since I was not paying attention, I almost walked through the glass window between the store and mall area. Both ladies smiled, saying they'd done that, too.

I realized I was nervous. Even though everyone who crossed my path was kind to me, the fears still played with my thoughts. It was important to remember that fear is often a lie, designed to keep us chained to what we think is safe, when, in reality, it keeps us from taking steps to really grow and reach our true potential. For me, fear was saying I was an imposter, a fraud, that any minute everyone would stop and point at me. It wanted to push me back into the closet, to again separate me from the rest of the world.

However, fear's grip was loosening with each public step I took as Susannah.

5

ESSAY: Imposter Syndrome and Being Transgender

Imposter Syndrome—One Trans Woman's Nightmare

A Personal Essay by Susannah Dawn

Imposter syndrome is real. It holds people back from living life to the fullest... from being able to fly. One can find many books, articles, and podcasts on the topic.

Basically, imposter syndrome is where a person seriously doubts their abilities in a given arena, and is therefore filled with self-doubt and the belief they are a fraud. That sentiment hinders their growth as they often focus unhealthy amounts of time and energy on worrying about what others around them think. It turns into a strong fear that people who know them will realize the truth: they were lucky to reach the positions they held. They worry about being "found out" as being less good at what they do than people thought. To make the situation worse, when someone with imposter syndrome receives honors for their achievements, they are likely to feel unworthy and are, therefore, unable to fully cherish the awards bestowed upon them.

Even with strong accomplishments, a person with imposter syndrome will believe they are living behind a flimsy façade. It's difficult for them to fathom they could be successful on their own merits, especially when they see "more legitimate" people around them doing the same things more capably, with greater knowledgeable and composure.

This hits home for many trans women. While I can't speak for everyone, for me it's difficult to not look over my shoulders in public, searching the faces of others around me while waiting for someone to point me out. It's the fear of being "read" by others and publicly identified as, and subsequently humiliated for, being transgender. There is also the trepidation of public ridicule due to other's observations and judgements of minor characteristics, like the fact that my physical body is larger than most (yet not all) cis women's. I worry I could fall back into my learned movement behaviors of fifty-plus years, which might betray me to be viewed as more masculine, even though I look like the lady I've always been on the inside.

Questions bounce through my head like lottery balls just before a big draw. Is my makeup right and proper? Does what I'm wearing fit right? Is it a little tight and thus, does it not look as smooth or feminine as it should? What about my walk? Do my shoes go with the outfit and, sometimes more importantly, am I walking naturally in them? Does my appearance explicitly state to anyone looking at me that I am truly a woman? Sure, it's likely that a lot of cis women have similar concerns; however, they are still less likely than I to be misgendered.

For me, imposter syndrome is a feeling of dread and self-doubt that although I look and feel like the woman I've known all my life that I am, someone might "discover" my physique hasn't always been female, and they might publicly scoff at and ridicule me.

However, imposter syndrome isn't something new in my life. It's been taking its toll on me for over a half century, poking at me in various ways.

From childhood, I felt like an imposter in my own skin, because I was required to identify as a male due to my body, my family, and the expectations of society. I knew I was a girl yet had to keep the true part of me hidden around other people, to act like someone I wasn't. It was not easy to open up to people and risk being teased, ridiculed, and bullied even more. I was able to play the charade of a boy, yet I wasn't happy. Thus, I was filled with self-doubt, feeling like an imposter in everything I did.

Wherever I worked, I only saw the mistakes I made and waited for others to see them as well, believing they would use them against me to show I was a phony, unworthy of my positions. The few times I heard anyone talk about me in a positive manner, I had difficulty believing there could be any truth to their words, as I only knew my mistakes.

With imposter syndrome, I simultaneously think I'm fooling everyone about my abilities while constantly looking over my shoulder, waiting to get caught. The reality is, the only person I'm fooling is myself. Feeling like an imposter, anxiously waiting to be uncovered in some horrendous and embarrassing fashion, I fail to realize the truth, a truth everyone else around me seems to already know: I'm awesome, I know what I'm doing, and I'm a woman who gets things done.

Towards the end of my first year of transition, I realized I no longer felt the strong tug of imposter syndrome while talking with my friends at Sephora. From every one of them, I experienced a sense of being one of the girls, a lady they've watched grow, develop, and become more confident in ways no one could have expected. I feel seen and accepted in the store, like any other lady who enjoys talking with, and learning from, her girlfriends.

The acceptance I feel around them isn't only focused on what we talk about. It's the way they speak with me. One associate always says, "Hey, Doll!" or, "How's it going, Doll?" when she sees me. Another beauty advisor often says, "Hey girl!" when I enter the store. Their words of greeting tell me I'm where I belong. There are the times I say something about my background, like mentioning that I played baseball in high school, or telling them I received an honorable mention in a writing contest for a story I submitted as Susannah, and it seems to catch them off guard as though they forgot I've only been out as Susannah for a short time. Those moments truly boost my confidence!

In many ways, it's because of my wonderful friends that I've been able to overcome the fear and anxiety of Imposter Syndrome, to step out of the dark closet into the public eye. From their love and support, my confidence grew exponentially. It's become easier to walk out of the house as my true identity. Before the fall of 2020, the thought of leaving the house wearing leggings instead of jeans, much less a dress, terrified me. When it finally happened, I was constantly observing my surroundings, searching for any signs I'd been read. Yet once inside stores, surrounded by friends, it was easy to drop the armor and enjoy shopping and asking questions of those associates I looked to for help with skincare and makeup. The more times I left the house wearing outfits I'd always known were right for me, the less intense the imposter syndrome became.

That's not to say my fears have totally departed. Quite often, in the mirror, no matter how much my face has changed from hormones and cosmetics, I still see the old "male" face trying to peek through. It sends a twinge of anxiety through me. Thus, there's an advantage to photographing my transition. Even though I may not like the earlier photos, they provide proof of just how much I've physically changed.

When speaking, I consciously put in the efforts to get my voice to the range and style that feels more naturally feminine. Yet I still fear talking with strangers. The tones I hear in my head when I speak often have some semblance of the voice of my past. The same phenomenon often occurs when listening to a recording of my voice. There's enough of the voice I grew up with to tell me my voice now is not quite where I want it to be. The result is a growing panic that my voice will "out" me.

These dysphoric aspects are disheartening to me, and seeing or hearing them builds up angst that I'll be negatively identified and ridiculed as an imposter. It was difficult to be happy living a life that pushed the true me down, identifying and living as a male due to my physique. I didn't like being told to "be a man" or to "man up" and do certain things. It hurt. My core is female, I am female, and the view of my soul has always been that God specifically made me this way to be in the world for His purpose.

Living as the woman I've always been made me happier and freer. I now live my life as my true self, a lady who is finally allowed to be out in the sun, relaxed and liberated.

Now that I'm out in the world, imposter syndrome still tries hard to rear its ugly head. I'm making new connections, in some cases, new friends who don't know my full history. They accept me for who I am. Yet, there are times when we exchange notes and someone asks a question I can only answer honestly by outing myself. Then the fear roils up inside; I want to answer in a transparent fashion, to let my truth out, yet I worry I'll lose a new friend. I end up spending more time crafting my response than is really necessary, feeling anxiety while wondering if they will respond, and if so, will it be positive? Receiving affirming replies, seeing that we are growing a connection, is what helps dispel my self-doubt in those situations.

I'm hit with those same worries when I consider becoming active in a women's community where I don't know anyone. It might be a women's book club, and I want to actively participate, to overcome my introversion. However, fear whispers in my ear, holding me back and telling me no one will accept me once they learn about my past. I worry that letting the truth come out will only embarrass me, since they'll view me as an imposter. Still, there are many women who have learned my story after and provided me with wonderful, positive feedback. While the fear tries to hold me down, other women are stepping in to help me rise.

Imposter syndrome took its toll on this trans woman. For years it scared me into submission, guaranteeing that if I exited my dark closet, I would be ridiculed, physically harmed, and filled with regret for having stepped away from the safety of that cold lonely space. However, friends I never expected populated my path, filling it with love and support. They never pushed me to come out any further than was comfortable, yet they encouraged me to take every step beyond my comfort zone to reach the spot I'm in today. I thank the Lord for each and every one of them. It seems the best way to overcome imposter syndrome, at least for this trans woman, is to trust the words of encouragement from the true friends who were placed in her life. I could never have made it this far without the initial, wonderful love and support I received from the beautiful people at Sephora. They became like family to me. They are the ones who helped me spread my wings and fly.

6

I'm Coming Out

By early February, it was still only the five women closest to me who knew about Susannah. I said nothing to anyone else, in or out of my family. My expectation was that the revelation would end many relationships and invite negative words to be fired at me. If that happened, then those words would be like a missile attack from which only the armor of God could keep me safe.

There was one person, though, who I decided to risk telling about Susannah: Cindy.

I'd known Cindy for almost fourteen years. We met in a graduate-school business program, and since it was a small class, everyone knew everyone. My friendship with her really began during a class "bonding" trip before the program formally started. During one of the segments of "team-building" activities, we began to chat and found common interests. When I was having an especially difficult time during the overseas class trip, she was the first person I spoke to who actually sounded like she cared about the problem I was dealing with, an issue that had me feeling down for much of that journey.

As the thought of coming out to someone I knew grew, the only logical name that kept coming to mind was Cindy. We weren't exactly close, with time and much of a continent between us, however, I followed some of her online posts and we'd exchanged a couple messages over the years. Something inside me said she was the one person I could trust and be transparent with about being a trans woman. For a few days I contemplated what to say and drafted two emails: the first, to open the door about asking her a personal question; and the second, what I wanted to say in the "coming out" email. When her response to the question was an enthusiastic yes, I sent the second email letting her know I was transgender, and she was the first person from my past I was coming out to. Even though I knew her background and trusted her based on how we got along in school, I was still nervous.

It was a long email that included several side notes to catch her up on some other aspects of my life before I worked my way to telling her I was transgender. I mentioned that the story I was working on focused on a trans woman named Candace who was the "first transgender combat (cavalry) officer in [a] future universe I am designing." I connected the main character with myself, telling Cindy, "In many ways, the story of Candace is about me (did Diana Ross' big song just start playing in your head?)... I actually fall under the T in LGBT (pretty much all my life)." The song was, "I'm Coming Out."

I also wrote, "I have been blessed that the very few people (outside of family) I have met who know about me have been very positive and helpful. God put them in my path, and for that I am ever so thankful."

Once the "send" button was pushed, my anxiety grew. I had just told a friend I was a trans woman, and there was no way to get the message back. While I believed Cindy was safe, fear would whisper, "What if you're wrong?"

Cindy's response was warm and positive. Though we didn't get to really connect much due to her schedule at the time, she was the only person beyond my wife and children to know me both before I considered transitioning and as Susannah. It was over a year before I told the second person. Our correspondence over the next few months was sporadic, and due to the stay-at-home protocols, there wasn't much to update, anyway. When June and July rolled around, I began to stay in touch with her more often. Part of that was due to her becoming one of the first to know when I began hormonal replacement therapy (HRT). By autumn and winter, I shared updates regarding what was happening with me as well as photos of how my change through the transition process was going. Cindy was my first big supporter.

Besides telling Cindy about Susannah, in February I began to reach out to others in the trans community. I was alone, and the trans community was something alien to me. Yet my path was moving towards transition, and I thought it would be nice to have connections within the community. At that time, I only knew one trans woman: Josie from MAC. It was a difficult step to take, reaching out to total strangers and hoping there would be an opportunity to actually talk with others in the transgender community. I was starting to view different YouTube videos of some who might be considered trans women influencers, but to be able to have exchanges with trans individuals was a direct way for me to learn more about the community itself.

When I tried to connect with others, unfortunately, there were either no responses, or a moderate response that failed to provide me with a feeling of safety and inclusion. Through LinkedIn, I sent connection requests to a handful of transgender activists near me. It was a gamble, hoping to find someone intelligent and willing to talk with me. No one responded.

I also sent emails to organizations, both local and national. I contacted two local LGBTQ organizations that stressed being open and safe environments to meet. I wrote messages to an organization's executive director and to a contact focused on the trans community. There was no response from the director. It seemed my query was not important enough to pass to someone within the organization who could respond. Although the trans community contact person did respond, it was a brief message that only said what the group was and when they met. Being an introvert and having a hard time taking those steps to reach out in the first place, there was no feeling of welcome or safety in the message. There was nothing to help me believe attending one of their meetings would truly be a safe place. It was a sterile response. I chalked it up as a failed option. As for the second group, while the response tried to sound positive, my gut reacted to something undefinable within the message, sensing that they felt unreliable.

I also sent a message to the transgender director of a national organization. In my email, I noted wanting to talk about how trans characters could be portrayed in stories, and to let them know I was a storyteller and wanted to help the community. There were no responses to the emails I sent in February and April. It became apparent, at least in my case, there was no safe place a fifty-something trans woman could turn to for assistance in stepping out of the confines of her closet and into the world. True, there were numerous options, yet first and foremost, this introverted woman needed to feel safe, and that wasn't happening.

The truth was, although I didn't know it at the time, the ladies at MAC and the associates at Sephora were my truest support group in helping me navigate the treacherous waters of coming out. It would be another four months before the closet door would open any wider. With their positive encouragement, eventually, I would take the first big steps to move out of the darkness, into the light. Before that could happen, however, there was February, March, and the subsequent stay-at-home months.

7

Before the Stay-at-Home Requirements

Outside of coming out to Cindy, February and March were a quiet time for me. Kim moved a thousand miles away in early February. From that point forward, I was home alone.

My first Sephora trip in February was with Kim. She wanted to visit the store before she left, as there was a lipstick she wanted for when she arrived at her new home and began to meet people. After she decided on the color, we walked around the store as she showed me other items she liked. Though she planned to buy the lipstick herself, I bought it for her as a gift to say "thanks for being with me as I took my many small steps out of the closet," and to wish her good luck in her new home.

I only purchased one other item in February. My fears and introversion held me back from visiting the store or asking the beauty advisors for help. Most store visits at that time included keeping my blinders on. Although I'd look for a face I recognized, I was simultaneously afraid of how I looked and how other people might be looking at me—especially those who could be trying to unravel my identity.

I still worried about what customers and others might think when they saw me. Even when it felt like I blended into my surroundings, there was no one to confirm it for me. Fear always poked at me as if to say, "Everyone around you sees what you're doing and knows you're not a real woman... you're just a pretender, and should go back to hide yourself away in that safe closet." Although I was certain my fear was wrong, it was still hard to ignore.

In my effort to hide in plain sight, my makeup remained simple and light while my outfits were fairly neutral. Trying to evade imposter syndrome, in public I kept my lipstick as close to my natural lip color as possible. My attire was comprised of jeans, sneakers, sweaters, and a simple jacket to cover myself up. It was important to wear clothes that made me feel like myself while simultaneously blending into the background in hopes that no one noticed me.

It was also a time when using the men's restroom began to feel awkward. My neutral appearance made it easy enough to go in, wash, and leave. Yet my hair was shoulder-length with a much freer-flowing style than most men wore. I had a growing fear that in those spaces, people would be close enough to notice my light makeup and lipstick. How would I explain it if someone questioned me? Shifting to use the single-room restrooms when possible helped to alleviate my nerves.

During my visits to the mall, I still looked for Joy in Sephora. However, it wasn't meant to be. She was never in, and per Sephora guidelines, no one could tell me when—or if—she might be in. Although some of the associates began to recognize me, like Brenda, none actually knew me. I haven't seen Joy since those first couple visits.

It was the end of February when I finally decided to begin facial electrolysis! I had a series of laser treatments for the darker hairs on my face a few years ago, though they weren't as successful as I'd hoped. Unfortunately, due to my age, there were a lot more white hairs than I ever expected, and those rascals tended to ignore the laser. I was tired of shaving every day, so I visited an electrolysis clinic where they would zap individual hairs with a jolt of electricity to kill the root and stop the growth permanently.

My first two appointments were on the last two days of the month, during which I chose to have them focus on the area around my mouth. I felt that if I wasn't able to do a lot of electrolysis, or had issues with the pain, it was best to start with what seemed like the worst area. Electrolysis turned out to be a much slower process than desired. Those first two appointments combined only managed to make one pass over my upper lip. It's amazing how many hairs were in that area of my face. It was excruciatingly time consuming to find, grab, and zap each one!

There were two different technicians. While I met one at my previous consultation appointment, it was the other lady with whom I had my first appointment. She would start the process for me.

When I entered her office and took off my coat, her first question was, "How long have you been on hormones?" In all fairness, part of me felt good hearing those words.

"I'm not," I said slowly. While I hadn't yet started HRT, I had used some this should be over-the-counter cream products that managed to increase my bustline a bit, for which I was happy.

When our time was up, she had barely done half of my upper lip. The next day I had an appointment with the other technician, and she completed zapping my upper lip.

The process had begun, yet knowing how costly it could become, I also began to pluck out the hairs around my mouth. My technique was similar to using an epilator, which plucked hairs out with little tweezers as a high rate of speed. The more I epilated my legs and arms, the less it hurt in those areas and the less the hair grew back, though the process was not an option for my face. "So," I reasoned with myself, "the same should happen if I start plucking hairs around my mouth between visits." What I didn't know was that I would have just one more visit for electrolysis before the shutdown began. The appointment lasted long enough for the technician to do most of the area under my bottom lip. After that, I often resorted to tweezers to remove the darker hairs. It was a positive feeling to find there was some truth to my theory that plucked hairs get lighter and, ultimately, stop growing.

Without electrolysis, I began searching for other options to permanently remove facial hair. There was, indeed, a product out there designed to help reduce, and ultimately eliminate, facial hair growth. It had two parts. The first was the "beard remover," which remined should be reminded me of other cream hair-removal products, while the second was a "growth inhibitor." At the start, I used the products sporadically through the spring and into the summer. Unfortunately, they were not designed for immediate results, but required persistent applications. Eventually, I saw results that confirmed they were slowly working. By fall, I changed my routine to use the beard remover once a week, while I used the growth inhibitor daily after shaving. Although still a slow process, it produced noticeably positive results. I had less morning stubble.

The first week of March included attending a conference focused on green schools. While I traveled to attend the same conference the previous year, this year it was located close to home. The downside was that conferences weren't a great place for the introvert in me to shine. I always found it difficult to meet strangers and begin conversations. That conference was no different. I talked with some of the people at the exhibit tables, though it was difficult to mingle and connect with other attendees. Observing the various groups of people in the halls, I felt that many already knew each other and often hung around together. It never felt safe to me to join a group and start talking, even though the people may have been open to such conversation. It was a problem I'd had since childhood, especially after I receded into my closet. Over time, those hesitancies crossed over into all social activities. I expected and feared rejection, which ultimately kept me quiet.

It's possible some of the difficulty at the conference was as simple as my hairstyle. While I've always wanted long hair, it was only during the past few years that I grew it out. I was still learning to manage and take care of it. During my youth, my dad cut our hair. He had the final say on length and style. Once I entered the military as an officer, there was the obvious requirement to keep haircuts short. After the military, I tried to let it grow, yet even with the help of a stylist, my hair refused to cooperate. It was not yet the right time to grow my hair long.

In April 2017, after coming out to Kim about being transgender, I stopped cutting my hair. Low and behold, it began to grow. From that experience, I also understood the need to really want long hair. It was a long growing process with many awkward periods where my hair just didn't look good. During the three-and-a-half years of letting it go, my hair grew about ten to twelve inches. Yet even as it grew, I was never quite sure how to take care of it. By March of 2020, it was down below my shoulders, and not entirely well groomed.

Even so, I trudged on through the conference, learning what I could and trying to make new connections. At the same time, the specter of COVID was everywhere. Although masks were not required at the conference, there was a lot of social distancing and arm bumps, which added to my feeling that people who already knew each other preferred to stay in their own clusters. Although I enjoyed what I learned, it was not as productive as I'd wished. I was uncomfortable and kept my distance from the other attendees. As an introvert, I felt safer to withdraw and observe than I did to risk bothering people. Thus, I was relieved not to have to interact with strangers any longer when the conference was over.

Throughout that period, when I was initially trying to step outside as myself, I spent a lot of time conversing with God about my path and direction. I was making sure I was where He wanted me to be. He often responded by putting specific, affirming pictures in my thoughts.

In early March, during one such conversation, I began to think about Josie, who was becoming a friend at the mall. I understood God was always with me, yet He also created us to have friends and communities. While I had a small core of family, it was difficult to remember having any friends during my life. Josie, however, had become a friend at a time when I simply needed someone who was willing to listen. Her patience when I talked went a long way to help me change and grow. When I visited the store and it was quiet, I had the opportunity to talk with Josie and learn about her and some of her views. With her, I had the chance to be honest about my journey, and Josie never interjected as I spoke. She was relaxed as she listened, seeming to know when to provide feedback and when to just let me talk. She was also the last person to give me a hug before the stay-at-home orders came down from the state. After that hug, I was isolated.

8

Life Alone during
Stay-at-Home Period

By mid-March, when the governor ordered all residents to stay at home unless they were critical workers, what little social life I had, visiting new friends at mall stores, ended. I had no one outside of family to contact. Even within family, except for my wife and youngest daughter, there was little contact. Being alone created a need for some type of routine to avoid letting the hours run into days, then run into weeks, without any clear delineation of time.

It seemed the entire pandemic was geared against me, forcing me to remain alone. I usually spent a week with my youngest daughter every spring break. A highlight of the year for me was often going with her to the zoo, a nature park, and sometimes the beach. However, 2020 cancelled them all. She's an important part of my life, and the loss of our time together hurt. All I could do was hope we'd still get our summer break together.

Thus, for the first six weeks, I stayed inside my home. When the weather cooperated, I'd go for a morning run. Otherwise, my only time outdoors was to check the mail. Except for a few calls with my wife or daughters during those couple of months, I didn't speak or text with anyone. I did, however, often send prayers out to people I knew. Knowing them was one thing, yet the introvert in me never felt those connections were close enough to reach out to, to see how they were doing and whether there was potential for more than a superficial friendship.

Not knowing any of my neighbors became an advantage as my budding transition slowly crept into my runs. About three times per week, I was up and out the door around daybreak. I began to wear what felt like more gender-appropriate clothing for me, with jackets and leggings to stay warm when I went out. I tied my hair back into a ponytail, and went off for a four-mile run. Those runs were the first times I went outside as my true self. Few people were out at that time of morning, and those who were seemed too focused on their own exercise to pay any attention to me.

Early on, I felt nervous going out. Some of my neighbors probably noticed the changes in my outward characteristics. My hairstyle and running outfits made evident that I wasn't hiding anything about being a woman. Thus, I searched for any signs that someone looked at me in a strange way. Sometimes, that small voice in my thoughts tried to make up problems where they didn't exist. As I approached others on the running paths, if they stepped off the path, moved to another sidewalk, or headed in some other direction, that voice said they didn't want to be near someone like me. I reminded myself people were social distancing and moving out of each other's way due to COVID fears. If the voice persisted, then my blinders went on to silence it.

I tried to keep busy writing on different projects while simultaneously searching for freelance writing opportunities. During the days, it was easy to fall into a habit of eating lunch while watching the 1970s live-action Saturday-morning shows I'd grown up with. The length of one show, about twenty-two minutes, was the right amount of time for a break. But when the show was over and lunch done, I got sucked into watching various YouTube videos, often news focused, telling myself I could watch just a couple short videos that looked interesting. That failed. Instead of adding about ten to fifteen minutes to my lunch break, too often, it became an hour or more of lost time. That made it even more difficult to get going and focus on my projects in the afternoon.

When the time came to finally leave the house to get groceries, the mask requirements made it easier to go out as myself. Having a mask over the lower half of my face enabled me to hide an area that bothered me: the shape of my lower face had jowls that seemed too big and square for a woman, and I lacked noticeable cheekbones. Since beauty was in the eye of the beholder, to me, the areas of my face that looked too masculine detracted from my ability to see my physical form aligning with who I really was.

Even though my outfits remained fairly neutral, I still maintained a more feminine appearance. Unfortunately, there were times when I had to deal with painful misgendering comments—incidents that caused fear and panic in me and threatened to stall my progress and send me back into my closet.

One specific instance was a trip for groceries. Entering the store, my coat accentuated my female curves, my nails were painted red, and my speech was a more feminine tone and manner. I stayed away from making eye contact with people as I shopped, enjoying the ability to walk through the store as myself. During checkout, the cashier said the appropriate words to acknowledge my appearance. However, the lady who bagged my purchase did not. She gruffly said, "Would you like plastic bags, sir?"

Whether her use of the word was intentional or accidental I couldn't know. What mattered was how that one word felt like gut punch, forcing all the wind out of me. Before she spoke, I was feeling good about myself. After her painful misgendering comment, I wanted to leave the store as quickly as possible, go home, and crawl into bed.

Even though everyone else in the store seemed to accept me for who I was, the words and tone of voice from that one specific woman hurt. In one individual interaction with her, my concerns about how others saw me, and my fears of never being able to blend in, built-up. Her gruff nature was like sandpaper, exposing old wounds from my dad's comments. I walked into the store feeling confident in who I was, and left in dismay with lowered self-esteem.

It's funny how as kids we're told a simple nursery rhyme to teach us that names and words don't hurt people: "Sticks and stones may break my bones, but names will never harm me." The thing is, words *do* hurt.

How would a bride feel if her parents told her she should have bought the other wedding dress just before her dad walked her down the aisle? The tears shed would no longer be from happiness; they'd be tears of sadness, dismay, and disappointment from what people she loved said on her important day.

Until that store visit, I was fortunate to rarely deal with someone misgendering my identity. There were two specific times it occurred, and both involved TSA at security points in airports. Before going through the body scanner, agents select which sex the machine should scan for. The machines are programmed to note differences between the two. To be fair, one encounter was a positive experience. My hair was longer, though I wasn't actively looking to pass as a woman. In that instance, after going through a scanner, it identified my chest as a questionable area. The gentleman who watched the scanner asked me if I'd rather have a woman pat me down, implying he realized I was inappropriately scanned. Because of his sincerity in asking, I told him it didn't matter. The pat down was fine, and I continued into the airport.

The second time, however, was extremely uncomfortable. Like before, my appearance was androgynous enough that it was a flip of a coin whether I'd be scanned as male or female. On that occasion, they scanned me at the security point as "male." Again, my chest area lit up on the screen. The male TSA agent gruffly groped my chest area, which felt both painful and demeaning. I went to the supervisor station to report it, pointing him out to the TSA lady who spoke with me. My voice was male enough that I didn't mention anything about being transgender—at the time, I hadn't made any decisions regarding transition. Therefore, the excuse I used when speaking with her was that there were men who had breast tissue, and the agent's actions were extremely rough. I told her I'd worry should he somehow end up patting down a female. The TSA lady was appreciative of my comments and said she would take care of it.

Being misgendered, even with a mask on due to COVID, was a very uncomfortable experience. It's a fear that's always concerned me when I was out. I tried to reason with myself that, even with a femininely decorated face mask, makeup (especially around my eyes), and a feminine build and outfit, it was still possible to be misgendered. Yes, my hands might be larger than most cis women, yet they were also comparable in size with some of the awesome ladies I'd met at Sephora. Still, if someone like me walked through the store looking like any other cis woman, speaking like a woman, and acting like a woman, there would be no reason she should be identified as anyone other than a woman. That made being misgendered even more painful.

In April, I learned through a social-media post that Josie had left town to move closer to family. At the time, there were only two ladies with whom I had any type of ongoing friendship: Josie and Linda. Knowing Josie was moving, and I was not likely to see her again in person, was difficult. It was hard enough for me to trust people, yet she quickly become one of those few I was comfortable confiding in. She always encouraged me to be my true self and talked with me in the store as she helped with makeup tips. Her friendship was a highlight of February and early March. She was both the first non-related person to hug me as Susannah, and the last to do so before the stay-at-home orders began. I sent her a couple emails wishing her well and kept her in my prayers.

My birthday popped up shortly after the news about Josie. The day itself was no different than most years, remaining quiet. Except for a couple calls with family members, there was no other interpersonal contact. I was used to that. Even in work or school environments where birthdays were celebrated, mine was usually the one overlooked. Taking the day off for myself, I baked a cake with one of my favorite cake-mix-and-frosting combinations, made a bacon-and-macaroni hot dish—one of my favorite comfort foods, and watched movies.

Though I was used to being alone, it still hurt. The shutdown period highlighted my not having friends to socialize with or contact if things weren't going well. In part, from the start of middle school, I interpreted the actions of people around me to mean that I wasn't important. It was difficult to figure out how to make friends, though again some of that was from interpretations of past experiences. I was never good at superficial conversations. My mind often drew a blank. Topics other people used to start and maintain basic conversations were often lost on me. Plus, for me, there needed to be a level of trust when making friends, an opening up to each other for the friendship to develop. More often than I'd like to admit, I was transparent with someone about how I was doing only to realize I put my trust in the wrong person and got hurt. That included times when something I said came back at me after going through a third-party's inter-pretation, usually in family situations, like the example with my now-ex mother-in-law. Those situations were uncomfortable, having my thoughts and words weaponized against me. It became best to not to let people in anymore—not even family members. If I didn't talk with anyone, there was no way to keep getting hurt by them.

While no friends meant not getting hurt, it also meant no one with whom to talk or exchange messages. There were a handful of people I had known over the years, yet those connections had never felt strong enough for me to be comfortable reaching out and starting a chat out of the blue. Plus, the few people I knew best were thousands of miles away dealing with their own situations during the pandemic. My fears and low esteem made me feel like I would be impeding on them and their time.

I saw people using social media posts to keep in touch. Yet to even consider doing my own posts wasn't easy. I didn't grow up with such technology. To think people cared if I went to a specific restaurant, passed through a specific airport, or was upset my favorite team lost on what felt like a stupid play, was alien to me. I often felt I could cut communication with the outside world and no one would miss me or, for that matter, even remember me.

However, that had changed over the last four months of 2020 going into 2021. I began to realize how the ladies at Sephora and MAC were as close to real friends as I'd ever had. They talked with me like I was part of the family. The few I opened up to a couple of times when I was on an emotional roller coaster would check in on me when they saw me in sub-sequent store visits! Those were the types of actions friends did for each other, and they'd never happened in my life. They became the only people I knew and felt like I could trust when having a hard time. They treated me like a friend: they were happy to see me and worried if I wasn't doing well.

To keep my thoughts off my lack of friends and social life, in April and May I started a major project that took up much of my time. Having something to occupy my thoughts was nice, especially when the ability to see people was limited. Another advantage was that the project's completion didn't require talking with people. I spent time on my project without feeling pressured by a deadline or people constantly contacting me about the status. The project helped make those months pass much more easily than they began.

Unfortunately, each day felt the same, which increased the potential I'd lose track of time. I used online church services to mark the weeks, so they didn't run into each other. I could count on them to occur at a specific hour each week, which in turn kept the weeks from turning into an endless line of days. Without something as simple as that break in the week, I could easily lose track of time and space.

As my transition progressed during that first year, I realized that even though I enjoyed the services and pastors of the church I'd attended for over a decade, I might not return to the building for in-person services. I don't know their overall position on transgender people, and asking such a charged question could unintentionally out me to my dad. He wasn't yet one of the family members who knew about Susannah. By mid-2021, only four people who knew me before transitioning also knew about Susannah, and none of them knew my dad. While church services were the keystone for me to set a fixed regular schedule, they were also an important aspect of my spirituality. Every step I took through my transition included God, and I didn't want to lose my ability to attend church, even if it was only online.

One area of transition I knew needed positive development was my voice. If I was truly going to step out when stay-at-home orders lifted, improving it to come across as more female was critical to my wellbeing. In May, I began a series of five video lessons devised to do just that. "Correcting" the sound emanating from my mouth was a key focus, as it was one of the stigmas that held me back from considering transition in the first place. My normal voice had lowered a bit over the past decade and was sure to be the first thing to out me if it wasn't adjusted, especially during a time when masks were required in public. My goal was to successfully complete each lesson over a five-week span. Though it sounded easy, it was harder than I expected. Part of my practice time included going over all previous lessons each day before doing that week's lesson. With simpler exercises, I had to knuckle down to give them the respect and attention they deserved. Accomplishing the more difficult lessons took more practice time. Although the process was slow, the practice was important. I wanted to train my vocal cords to get into the lower end of the female range as soon as I spoke, then continue to refine my voice from there.

Initially, it took significant concentration to get into the lower feminine range. After about a month, it became easier to speak there "on the fly." That was the encouragement I needed. Once speaking in my goal range became second nature, I moved into a slightly higher tone in a more natural fashion. Being home alone provided ample opportunity to speak aloud to myself in those higher ranges. It felt awkward at the start, talking to thin air, yet my overall voice improved. The process helped me gain confidence in myself to go out as Susannah when the stay-at-home restrictions were lifted.

9

ESSAY: Why Now?

Why Now?

A Personal Essay by Susannah Dawn

For over half a century, my life has been at odds between me—the person I am at heart, and my body—the form into which I was born. Yes, I learned to understand and live with my body as others viewed it, growing up with it—in it. However, it was never a true picture of the real me, the beautiful person who actually lived inside of it. I was never comfortable in that physique. My own body didn't align with my feminine self, my soul, if you will.

When I was born, I can envision the doctor taking a glance between my legs, followed by some of the first words my little ears would hear, "Congratulations! It's a boy!" My parents were so happy at the news. Throughout my life I heard Mom tell people how glad she was that all her children were boys, often complaining that girls were much harder to raise.

As for my father, he was excited to learn his first born was a son. It meant his legacy and family name were secure. Having a boy provided him with that "little me" to whom he could teach all the things he enjoyed. Most likely, he thought, or at least hoped, his son would grow up to be like him: a chip off the old block.

However, nothing would be further from the truth.

Well before starting school, as early as age two or three, I remember going to bed every night saying the same prayer: "God, please let me wake up a girl." By that age, I knew there was a difference between boys and girls, though not the specific details. It was clear to me I belonged with the girls, because inside I was one of them. At such an early age it was obvious something was not right in my life, an error which needed to be corrected—hence the nightly prayers. I also understood at a very basic level how being a girl was the only way to feel true to myself.

That prayer never went away. Every so often I said it before falling asleep. As I got older, saying the prayer popped into my thoughts when something I saw in the mirror bothered me. Maybe my face looked too square, too masculine, or I felt I was too flat and wanted my body to develop feminine curves instead of what I saw as a rigid, stiff, male physique. When I saw a feature in me that appeared more masculine than feminine, it hurt. If that was what I looked like, how could I consider going out in public as the person I was created to be on the inside? Knowing the truth of who I was, it hurt to be trapped looking like someone else.

Therefore, I lived life based on the appearance of my body. It grew increasingly difficult over time. Society said anyone who looked like me was a boy, case closed. To step out and act otherwise was wrong and subjected me to teasing, ridicule, bullying, shaming, and the possibility of physical harm or even death. I understood those first four very well. I suffered each one at various times during my life: parents, classmates, on the school bus, and my ex-spouse. The hurt piled onto a growing mountain of pain that made basic social situations agonizing. I was unable to let family members know about personal issues, as they often went behind my back and told other people what I said. I was confronted with my own words, filtered by a third party. My trust in family members diminished. I learned it was in my best interest to stay quiet and keep everyone out—to become an introvert and spend most of my time alone. When that reality sunk in, it became almost impossible to open up and develop honest, deep, real friendships with anyone. Though I needed true friends to hang out with and share the ups and downs of life with, such relationships were out of reach.

I yearned to live according to my true self, my female soul that was carefully hidden in a body viewed otherwise. The idea of transitioning my form to match the real me ebbed and flowed throughout my life. The need to be myself, to go out into the world as the woman I knew I was born to be, was always strong. And yet, at those times when I thought I was ready to look into transitioning, fear always reared its ugly head. For half a century, fear's grip forced my resolve to melt away and kept me from taking those first steps.

Defining each fear was like navigating a series of rapids for the first time, never knowing what to expect. Some fears were about avoiding the obvious: verbal abuse such as ridicule, teasing, shaming, and being targeted by bullies. Each one hit close to home. When I first tried to exhibit my female side in my early youth, my father used spankings and ridicule to put such thoughts out of my head. He would tease me any time I showed interest in something he thought was for girls. After entering middle school, I became the target of bullies, though I never understood why. Maybe it was because I was alone with no friends on the playground. In the end, looking back over my life, it surprises me, how much abuse I received.

Other fears revolved around the terminology of the times. In the 1980s and 90s, *transsexual* was the common term for someone looking to transition to become a woman. While I can't speak for everyone who knew their true self didn't align with their body during those years, for me, *transsexual* was not a flattering term. The uncomfortable sexual connotations attached to it produced negative feelings inside me when I saw the word. The topic itself seemed to be pandered on talk shows purely for ratings. Rarely was the intention to understand trans people, to show that they were good people who only wanted to live normal lives like everyone else. That one word created a negative sense inside me. It fed my fears, keeping me locked in an undesired figure so I wouldn't even consider exploring transition options.

So, why now, at my age?

Why has the desire to actively transition my body to match the person I've always known I am become so urgent? There is so much I'm likely to lose should I actually take the necessary steps and go through with it.

For one thing, many of the people in my life are likely to leave. Let's be honest: being an introvert, I have very few close friends. However, I have a number of acquaintances and it's difficult to predict which people will leave. The only way to confirm such fears is to transition. On that path, some of those I expect to leave will do just that. Other acquaintances who I've thought or hoped would be part of my life may decide to no longer have anything to do with me. Is transitioning now worth the possibility of losing people who seem to have value and importance in my life?

Then there's family. It's difficult to believe any blood relatives, save maybe one or two, would not turn away from me. I know their backgrounds. During family get togethers it's hard not to hear their comments, opinions, viewpoints, and stereotypes. They say nothing to hint at tolerating and supporting anyone who is transgender, much less accepting them. Most of the family members who I believe would support me have passed away. It's my immediate family by second marriage and adoption, a number I can count on one hand, who have shown positive support of who I am and my transition.

The ability to find work could also be more difficult or even impossible. It's always possible that people or an organization might judge or be prejudicial towards transgender people, no matter the stated HR policies. HR would learn about me through the company's background checks. If hired into a prejudicial environment, I would either have to bear the difficulty of the situation and try to survive it or leave and try to find someplace new.

Then there's always the chance I could be publicly "outed" and even attacked. It seems to be in the news all the time. The possibility of mental and physical harm is real, especially if I crossed paths with a transphobic person who decided to choose me as their target. The things they could say in public would be filled with venomous hate, designed to tear me down and publicly shame and humiliate me. Should they become violent in such situations, it would be difficult to know if I would survive.

Yes, there are many reasons not to transition, to remain hidden within a form that looks wrong to me, the visage of a stranger. That is the "safe" approach to life. However, all those reasons pale compared to the key reason to transition: there is even more to gain by going through with it.

My life becomes a clean slate. It's a time when I can start over and be who I was born to be, to live as the woman I've always known I am in my heart. Though who I am from the outside changes, transition does not affect my experiences in life: they are, and always will be, mine. Being a writer, opportunities may be different, yet they are sure to be more exciting and fit my real passions. I am a better writer when I enjoy what I'm doing and do it as my true self.

Although many friends and acquaintances will be lost, new friends will be gained. Some will be in the transgender community. Many of the people I meet there will have shared experiences with me, while others will consider themselves allies. Then there will be those who come from various places outside that community, people whose paths I cross in everyday life, the flower of friendship just blossoming between us. There are so many people out there who are good in their hearts, who will help build up lives instead of trying to tear them down. And I want to do the same for them, which is what real friends do. I know there are new friends out there, people I've yet to meet, and a place for me in a wider community in this world.

Through all of this, my relationship with God remains strong. I take every step knowing that He is watching. I make every decision after taking it to Him in prayer. And I get it—there will be many who read those words and frown, believing it impossible for anyone to be both transgender and Christian. It should be equally obvious that I do not agree with them. Although I am not going into detail here, I will note that the Lord looks at the heart, not the outside appearance, which is different than how we tend to view each other in current societies. Thus, while it took me half a century to embrace who I am, I know He's known exactly who I am from the beginning and created me this way for a purpose.

Transition is a scary thing, yet for me it's also an opportunity to become complete. It's a chance to bring back the fun-loving and carefree person I was in childhood, before having my true nature stifled. The ability to publicly be the woman I've always been will make me whole and bring vibrancy back into me and my life. Transition will allow me to be a free and happy woman, similar to many of the women I know and observe who are outgoing and fun loving, living their lives to the fullest.

As a child, I could do nothing to stand up for myself. At a young age, I quickly understood there was no way I could tell my parents I clearly knew both who and what I was in this world, a girl. Their actions towards my girlish expressions started me on a path that was difficult to step off. However, I am now at the place where I *can* step off that painful path, forgive those who hurt me, find the ways to heal, and live life by following my heart and being the woman I've always known I was meant to be in this world.

One final note: this is the story of one transgender person… one out of millions. Many others have experiences similar to mine. They will stay in their own stifling closets, afraid to poke their heads outside due to the fear of what will happen to them, fear of having their lives destroyed just for being themselves.

I write this for those who need to read it, be they transgender or not. It's to tell a story of one, with the understanding that there are so many more stories out there to tell. As the words here will speak to many, my prayer is that they will provide a positive feeling in the reader, and an understanding and acceptance that each of us was designed uniquely, to be the person we are created to be, and to love each other as we want others to love us.

10

Going Out When Stay-at-Home
Was Lifted

By June, I slowly found ways to go out more often. Sure, it was still a struggle to go out when masks and pandemic fears were prominent. Yet, so much time was spent cooped up alone in my home, it was important that I start spending time out of it. I began simply by ordering takeout a couple of times per week. I stayed away from delivery services, both for cost and time. I also managed to increase my grocery shopping to about once a week, which doubled as a chance to "socialize" and be around other people. While Susannah was going out in small steps, it remained relatively safe.

Only during my morning runs through the neighborhood did I publicly expand my visibility as Susannah. Weather permitting, I ran a couple of times per week. As June rolled around, my running increased with the temperatures and longer daylight hours. I ran as early as possible each day. Over time I recognized the small group of people who, like me, took advantage of such favorable early mornings.

In the warmer weather, I needed to wear more suitable running outfits. Jackets did a good job hiding my shape in colder weather, but it quickly became too warm for long sleeves. Looser dark shirts became my primary choice to hide the curves of my chest area. It was frustrating to feel the need to stay hidden, yet the fear of being too open, too easy to potentially be "outed" by anyone was strong. I wasn't ready to wear the running attire I wanted, to truly come out to the world. I used a light tinted moisturizer or foundation—especially with a sunscreen application—to hide any redness from shaving and provide sun safety before heading out. Once my earphones were on, I headed out the door.

As the temperature went up, the length of my leggings shrunk. The next step was compression shorts with side pockets for my phone. My thought was, even in shorts, I was still hiding; anyone could run in compression shorts. So, the big step came towards the end of the summer when I bought my first pair of capri-length leggings. There was no way to view them as anything other than feminine, especially with the beautiful pink trim along the sides. Sure, I was nervous heading out the door the first few times, unsure what the neighbors might think... if any were up. However, I didn't know any of them, so there was no real reason to worry.

The capris were a breath of fresh air. The freedom that flowed over me was invigorating. Fortunately, I lived near open spaces that included nature venues, and I often looked around at the scenery. With the freedom I felt in my capris, the colors of the trees, the grass, and even the sky were more vibrant. Everything was more peaceful. My pace even improved!

As I mentioned before, some of the faces I saw during my runs became familiar, albeit from a distance. I tended to recognize other women, though it was hard to make eye contact with any of them due to my strong shyness around strangers. However, I was able to observe many from the corner of my eye. Some of the women began to recognize me, and even wave slightly as we passed. Those times often happened while on adjacent paths. Their simple wave made those days better, as I felt accepted for being me.

There was one woman who I often saw near an apartment complex. She usually walked her dogs around the same time each morning. She always had a large smile when she saw me. It was hard not to return her smile. Over time, the smiles turned into small waves, though I never stopped running to talk with her. Thinking back through my life, it's hard to remember a time I stopped to talk with a stranger in any setting apart from school, work-related situations, or conferences. I had no idea how to start a conversation and talk with people. Too often my concerns about starting conversations with people centered around not wanting to bother them. Whenever I talked to people I didn't know well, I sensed they were often looking for an opportunity leave our conversation to go find someone they'd rather talk with.

One sunny morning, I went for a walk to give my legs a rest from running. I passed the lady with her dogs on a small bridge over a creek along a local road. I wanted to say something, but my mind went blank, so I focused on the music in my headphones. We both said hi, which was the extent of the conversation. And, true to form, ideas of what I could have said came to mind half an hour after passing her.

It took another five or six weeks before we saw each other again. I was determined to talk with her. It was a really big deal for me, initiating a conversation of any length. I was running along the sidewalk on the same side of the road as her. Seeing me, she moved off the sidewalk towards the street as though planning to cross to maintain social distancing.

Out of the blue, I stopped and said in my best Susannah voice at the time, "I love your smile."

She also stopped. "You have a great smile, too."

Although the conversation was short, it was a major step for me. It opened the door that allowed me to feel safe enough to talk with her, should our paths cross again. Although it took time, in September we began to talk for a couple minutes at a time. It took that long partly due to not crossing paths very often. That first real conversation in September was, again, a walking day for me. We were near an intersection.

"I forgot your name," she said.

"Susannah," I replied, though I didn't remember telling her before. Then I said something I never expected: "I'm socially awkward, especially in non-work settings, so it surprised me when I spoke with you that first time when I said you have a great smile."

"That's surprising," she said, "as you have such great energy." Then, as a couple ladies ran past us, she said hello to them. Looking at me she continued, "I'm Latreese, though everyone calls me 'Brown' as it's my last name and easier for people to say."

Although I enjoyed talking with her, a couple different fears began to creep up inside. The first was my voice; even though she said nothing to cause my worry, voice fear was often the first to pop up. The second was an insecurity I'd had much of my life: when a conversation seemed to be going well, I worried I was taking up too much of the other person's time. So often, with family, colleagues, or schoolmates, I got a sense that they felt I was wasting their time and they'd rather be somewhere else. Latreese was always pleasant to talk with. If she had a time crunch and needed to get home for a meeting, she was always kind about letting me know she had to get going. I felt safer to stop and chat, knowing her time was valuable yet she'd talk with me when she could and let me know when she couldn't.

Except for seeing Latreese when I ran and exchanging a few video calls with my wife and daughter, June remained a quiet month, with one exception. I often reviewed a few transgender-focused news postings each day, and one specific article caught my eye. The impact of that one article would change my year... and ultimately, my life. It set me on a trajectory that I never truly thought was possible for me. It was the first story I saw about a digital health service focused on the transgender community.

11

And So, It Begins... HRT

During much of my life, the idea of starting hormone replacement therapy (HRT) was in the back of my mind. It was only during the past four years, after coming out to Kim, that I researched various HRT options around where I lived. My wife and I had conversed about it, though back then, the timing was not right. I prayed about it, seeking guidance for where my path was going. In 2017, the path was only to research the topic, as I considered what lay ahead for me.

In June of 2020, I came across an article about a company in the United States providing gender affirming care in many states, including mine. The article mentioned how the company was a trans-led medical provider focused on the transgender community. They operated as a digital health service with a membership approach and a monthly fee. They provided an alternative to seeing a formal physician where I lived.

I felt a door open for me to take the next step towards transition. I did more research. In June 2020, there were maybe a dozen states where their services were available. It was important to me to learn that the organization was founded by a trans-woman physician, and the medical aspect included scheduled blood tests, medication prescriptions provided by licensed medical professionals within each state, and regular check-ins with members.

After my research and lots of prayer, I filled out the application and made a video appointment to discuss my situation with one of the organization's local nurse practitioners. Potentially starting the HRT process was exciting, but also made me nervous. I wanted to make sure I did everything correctly and safely. I was also anxious about the video chat wherein I'd appear as my true self to a stranger. Her only knowledge of me was the forms I filled out. My emotions were truly mixed.

My video chat was on a Sunday afternoon at the end of June. That morning, I put on my foundation, eyeshadow, and lipstick, then selected a nice floral blouse. I felt good about my presentation, yet anxiously wondered what the other person expected of me during the call. When it began, she immediately put me at ease with her smile and honest demeanor. She was very personable, knowledgeable, and accepting of me. I asked questions, and felt she wanted to help me achieve my goals. She explained the program, talked about my medication options, and answered my questions. At the end of our conversation, she said she'd call in my prescription.

I was only days from starting HRT!

After the call, another mix of emotions flooded over me.

I was excited to begin the process to adjust my figure, to start a transformation that would allow me to look like the woman I've always known I am.

There was a deep-seated fear of how people I knew might react once they learned about my transition. There would come a point where my features—especially my face and the shape of my body—would change into a more feminine form that I could no longer hide. I worried about what the physical outcome would look like, especially as I was starting at a more mature age. Would my face transition remove all the "male" aspects I found frustrating?

I also felt relief knowing I was about to take the next step in my journey. I was to walk through a door the Lord opened for me.

The day I picked up my prescription was exciting! I considered taking my first pills on July fourth, viewing it as a momentous opportunity to celebrate Independence Day by starting my own independence. However, even with such a grand thought, I took the first dose on July first. My desire to start the next phase of my journey outweighed the idea of wait-ing. The first felt perfect to begin my transition.

Over the years, I'd taken a few over-the-counter products and used creams to try to start a transition, knowing there was never any guarantee I would be able to officially begin HRT. Because of that, I started with a few slight curves that many trans women don't have at the beginning. Plus, being a little older, I had a little more weight on me than if I'd started twenty years ago.

As July progressed, I found I began to feel more relaxed. My body adjusted to both the estradiol coursing through it and the T-blockers re-ducing the testosterone production. The mixture of the two created a calming presence that ebbed and flowed through my body. I began to smile more. A sense of openness that I'd lost in childhood slowly returned. While it would take time to overcome the introverted tendencies I har-bored and grew over the years, I felt a sense they might eventually erode, and that I would feel more like myself.

After two years of HRT, I reflected on changes I hadn't quite realized were occurring. I was feeling better physically and emotionally—steady, as I made my way through life. I was freer emotionally, as though I'd removed the strait jacket that was holding me down. I laughed and cried more eas-ily, and I could smile most of the time. The emotions I'd kept pent up most of my life were finally able to flow freely. Releasing those emotions also rid me of stress I'd accumulated through life. When I walked, my move-ments flowed in a more graceful manner, unlike the robot-like movements prior to starting hormones. I had spent my life being stoic, stiff, and un-able to relax and flow because that's how men were expected to behave. I never wanted to be that way. Inside, I was a relaxed and free-flowing woman, and during my months of HRT, I was gaining that part of me on the outside as well.

I understand some people think being transgender can be cured, though I know that's not true for me. I lived my life with plenty of testos-terone coursing through my system. It did absolutely nothing to counter the fact that, even through puberty, I knew I was a girl. Though God never directly answered my prayer to wake up the next morning as a girl, He did answer it in a very positive fashion.

I'm happy to be a trans woman. God allowed me to accomplish things that, in my era, cis women were not allowed to do, such as be a US Army Cavalry officer. Being in the cavalry was part of what shaped me. It gave me material and ideas for some of the stories I've written. Yet, even during those years in service, I still knew who I was at my core, and she was in no way aligned with the body in which I was encased. The girl in me has always been there, and she's grown up to be a woman. It was time for her to take the next step out of the darkness and into the light.

12

A Return to Sephora and Next Steps Out

In July, I made my first few trips to the mall. My outfits were primarily jeans, sneakers, and more unisex shirts. The mask requirements were actually a blessing for me. At the start of my transition, I had no idea how I actually presented in front of others. For half a year I'd been using moisturizer and wearing foundation around the house and on my few short excursions to the grocery store. I was excited to make that first trek to the mall as there were two locations I wanted to visit: MAC and Sephora. Because the MAC location was small, it was easy to see who was inside; if I didn't recognize anyone, I wouldn't enter.

As for Sephora, my experience before the closures was positive enough that I felt safe to enter the store even if I didn't know anyone. Once inside, even with the masks, I recognized a few associates from before the shutdown, but none were women I'd interacted with before. I found it difficult to talk with anyone during those first visits; the introvert inside kicked into high gear. When anyone asked if I needed help, I said, "I'm fine." With tunnel vision, I'd focus on products on the shelves, not associates available to help.

I wanted to talk with people, and sometimes hoped they might come back to check on me. However, after years of learning that it was safest to stay away from others, I couldn't overcome my fears. During most of July, I was never pressured to receive help, and no one said anything to me apart from kind offers to help if I needed it. I later learned that the associates told each other if a customer wanted to be left alone, which was probably the case with me. However, it also became obvious over time that many of the associates were beginning to recognize me, even though I wasn't yet comfortable talking with them.

At the end of the month, I finally asked for help to find a product. Betsy asked if I was looking for anything in particular. I told her I was unable to find the Clinique product I wanted. The product was not currently in the store, but she was kind enough to order it for me, and soon we started talking. Betsy became the first post-lockdown associate to find a crack in my shell. Through that small opening, she managed to let me know it was alright for me to be vulnerable and come outside. We talked briefly about the 80s, finding a common background that also helped me feel more comfortable around her.

On a subsequent visit, Betsy recognized me and came over to talk. It might have been a little thing for her, since she saw so many people in the store daily, yet for me it was a huge positive surprise that she remembered me. She stood about shoulder-height to me with dark shoulder-length auburn hair that she kept tied up in a ponytail or bun. She again asked in her always cheerful, bouncy manner if there was something she could help me find.

"I'd like to find a light, shimmery blue eyeshadow," I replied. "Something similar to the light and shimmery style of a few shades in the Fenty palettes I have." I showed her the style.

When she showed me a few selections, I said, "I'm not looking for blue shadow like from the 80s. Although it was popular back then, it's a bit more than what I'm looking for now."

She knew what I meant, and it became the start of a new friendship. Although Betsy took me around the store, there wasn't anything that fit the color and style I had in mind. However, what she did provide was a friendly face who helped me feel more welcome about entering Sephora.

My worries were still there, especially as I had no idea how others saw me when I was out in public. I had no one to talk with, no one to ask about how I looked, or whether I should change something to better present as the woman inside. Betsy helped me relax in Sephora. Her gentle nature aided me in my ability to open up.

While my connection with my daughter, Lauren, and her wife Allison slowly grew in June, July was when I truly let them in. Lauren offered to connect me with a friend of hers as she knew I wanted to expand my storytelling abilities. While the connection never materialized, I felt more willing to be transparent with Lauren about my background and how difficult coming out as a trans woman was for me. The note I sent her was, in her words, vulnerable. I was unfiltered about my past, including my difficulty connecting with other kids in middle school, my inability to make real connections with my family, and how I felt like the person stuck out in left field because of being transgender. Looking back, it was one of the most important emails I'd ever written, and it brought me closer to both of them.

Lauren offered to introduce me to another trans woman she knew, and I gratefully accepted her offer. That time the connection worked, and we've exchanged a few emails. It was nice to finally have another trans woman to exchange messages with, even if our notes were infrequent and she was considerably younger than me. It didn't change the fact we are both trans women who'd had many similar obstacles to overcome. I greatly appreciated her friendship.

While I had no luck trying to connect with other trans women and organizations earlier in the year, by August I had connected with two women. Lauren's friend was the first, and the second was a director of transgender equality in a southeastern state. When I sent a note to the second lady, she was willing to have a short phone conversation. We talked about her focus on transgender awareness and what she was doing in her organization. I told her I was finally stepping out and had begun HRT. Even though it was a short chat, it felt good to finally talk with another trans woman.

July was like a new beginning for me. I began HRT at the start of the month, returned to the mall, and began to make friends in Sephora. Life was beginning to look brighter to me, with new possibilities opening before my eyes.

13

August: a Month of Endings

August began like July ended.

When I visited Sephora, I enjoyed talking with Betsy. I began to pull back my personal blinders to see more than just the products on the shelves. I could tell there were good associates in the store; I just had to overcome the hurdles of my introverted feelings and try to talk with others. That my makeup application was rudimentary at best held me back; I worried about what others thought.

It was obvious to me that my skills with cosmetics were severely lacking. I always wanted to learn how to do my own makeup, to learn new ways to make my face look the best it could. It was important to walk outside with my makeup looking so good that no one could perceive I'd ever been anyone apart from smiling Susannah.

In mid-August, an important step towards becoming my true, feminine self occurred when I met Carol. When I saw her in Sephora, she reminded me of Joy. They were about the same height, and she had a similar streak of blue in her dark hair. The way she spoke with me, her tones and willingness to talk, helped me to feel safe around her. I could begin to relax and feel comfortable asking her any makeup question that ran through my head. My first question was about concealers. I felt a need, at times, to use something like that around my mouth and lower-face area due to shaving. As we looked for a concealer to meet my needs, Carol also showed me ways to put it on so it would provide the finish I wanted. The way Carol listened to me, helped me, and showed me how to use the products, made me feel comfortable asking her for help finding a new blush and setting spray. Carol's kindness helped me feel more comfortable in Sephora and set the groundwork for me to open up with other associates over the next few months. I was beginning to talk with new people.

Two days after that visit with Carol, my world crashed in around me.

This feels like the right moment to say that I chose my name because of my mom. Years back, I'd asked what name my parents would have given me if I'd been a girl.

"We would have named you Susan Dawn," Mom said.

I liked the name, especially as I'd always liked the name Susan. Yet, "Susan" was often shortened to Sue, which was a name I didn't want. I'd known some very nice Sues in elementary school yet wasn't fond of the ones I'd met in later years. That's when I decided on Susannah Dawn. It was still the same basic name Mom told me. However, there was something about the name *Susannah* that felt like it fit me. Plus, Kim decided the shortened version would be Suzie, which I loved.

My mom had Alzheimer's and had been living in a memory care facility for about five years. It was tough seeing her deterioration every time I went to visit. During 2020, COVID's stay-at-home / work-from-home orders prevented me from seeing her. The facility where she lived kept my dad updated on how she was doing, usually saying she was well. However, some issues occurred at the end of July and beginning of August that impacted her overall health. By the middle of August, the facility told Dad that Mom was sliding fast. They recommended hospice. Only a few days after she began hospice in the memory care facility, Dad was informed they didn't expect Mom to last more than seventy-two hours. My brothers were adjusting their schedules to travel, so they could see her the next day and spend time with Dad. I visited Mom that afternoon in her room.

Because no one knew about my transition, I removed all resemblance of Susannah before seeing Mom. No one said much to me while I was there. After signing in and having my temperature taken, I was brought to her room where it was just the two of us—me with my mask on and Mom asleep in her bed.

I knew this day was coming. I'd had five years to prepare for it. At the facility entrance, the visit felt like any other. I'd see my Mom, see how much she changed since my last visit, and get some time to be with her. When I entered Mom's room, I still felt fine.

Once alone with her, I spent the first few minutes watching her sleep. Her head was tilted over her right shoulder, facing the wall, and she made a light snoring sound. Her hair was curled into a cute bun just behind her left ear (and probably a similar bun on the right), reminiscent of Princess Leia, just smaller. I believed Jesus was in the room, standing there at the foot of her bed making sure she heard and knew what I said. While I spoke, she raised her head slightly, maybe an inch or so, a handful of times.

I wondered whether she might leave, pass away while I was still in the room. I tried not to think of that as I had no idea how I'd feel or what I'd do should she die while I was with her. I watched her for a few minutes before I left to make sure she was still breathing.

During my time with her, I said, "I love you, Mom," many times, as if trying to make up for the feeling that I never said it enough. Being alone with her provided me the chance to open up to her about the things I had to say, even if she already knew them. I started off with the toughest one.

"You probably already know this," I said. "I'm transgender."

I believe that was one of the times when she raised her head, as if to say, "Yes, Dear, I knew that. I am your mother, after all."

Once I told her that, it was easier to say the rest.

"Thank you for teaching me to bake and cook," I said, suddenly remembering when I won a baking contest in high school. "It was because of you that I won that baking contest with Gramma's snickerdoodles recipe... you taught me how to bake them.

I know I wasn't the best kid in the world," I continued. "I've always had difficulty talking with people—which included you, yet I always felt your love, which you gave freely and often. I'm so glad that you were my mom. You're the only person I wanted for my mom... you're the best mom."

I remembered my brothers were on their way and told her they'd be there to see her the next day. I hoped it would help her stay until they could say goodbye.

The cd player by her bed played Christian choral music. She loved to sing, and it was a recording of one of the choral concerts she was in a few years ago. When the disk ended, I restarted it from the beginning as it created the right ambiance for Mom.

When Mom's roommate returned to the room, that felt like my cue to leave. I knew I said what I needed to tell her. As I passed the front desk, I told the nurse, "my brothers are arriving later tonight and plan to see Mom tomorrow."

After leaving her, I went to see Dad to let him know how peaceful she was in the room. We talked for a bit before I returned home. I knew he'd also be getting ready for my brothers' arrival later that night.

It wasn't even two hours after I left Dad when he called me.

"Your mom's gone."

When he told me the approximate time they thought she had died, I realized she passed away shortly after I left... it was within an hour of when I left her bedside. I rushed through to the end of the call with Dad as it was hard to hold myself together. Once he hung up, I cried, and cried, and cried.

When I was able to compose myself, I started my own round of calls to let my wife and daughters know Mom was gone. Although my wife was sad, fortunately she was overseas with friends and family around her for support. My daughters also had others around them for support. My dad would have my brothers and their families with him for a few days, and my brothers had their wives and in-laws.

I, however, was on my own. There were no friends I could call and talk with as I rode the wild, emotional roller coaster of loss. I didn't want to worry my wife and daughters over what I was going through, feeling that having at least a thousand miles between us made things difficult enough. I knew they loved me; there was nothing else they could do for me.

Even though I was on my own, I immediately knew the one place where I could go, the one place that was safe for me, the place that would be able to keep some of the sadness at bay: Sephora. I had told Betsy that my mom was not long for this world. Thus, Sephora was where I went the day after Mom died.

When I entered the store, my blinders were on with the sole focus of finding Betsy. She not only accepted me from the first time I met her, but she also always seemed genuinely happy to see me. Betsy was the one person I needed to see that day, and when I found her, she was standing with someone I didn't recognize, but who would also become an important friend: Wendy.

"How are you?" Betsy said in her chipper voice when she saw me.

I was slow to answer. "Mom died yesterday." I kept the tears back as I recapped seeing Mom and how she passed minutes after I left her.

"We've both lost our mothers," said Wendy. The two women were about the same height, though Wendy had thick, darker-blonde hair that she often wore in a ponytail.

They took a few moments to talk with me and make sure I was doing alright. It truly felt like friends helping a friend, something I'd never experienced before. When Betsy had to go help another customer, Wendy stayed with me, talking with me as she helped me find a tinted moisturizer and a hair product.

During that same visit, when I saw Carol in the store, I thanked her for helping me find the blush earlier in the week. She then helped me find a new eyeshadow stick, a product I hadn't used before.

My visit to Sephora that day was what I needed... a place to go where I felt accepted and befriended. I saw other associates in the store recognize me. I felt their warm smiles, which provided an unspoken comfort on a day I sorely needed it. After that visit, I decided to complete the Sephora purchase survey online to thank the wonderful associates for their help, not knowing if they would actually see it. It was the first time I'd ever done the survey.

~~~~~~

**Actual Sephora survey comments from my store visit
after Mom passed away:**

The ladies who helped me made me feel welcome and accepted.

Carol was awesome as she helped me find a new eye shadow, and previously this week, she helped me find the perfect shade for a new blush.

Betsy and Wendy were a blessing! My Mom passed away the day before, so I came to Sephora trying to take care of myself and hoping to find ladies I knew. They were very empathetic when I told them about Mom and extremely helpful helping me find something for my hair and a tinted moisturizer.

Also, there were other ladies who I recognized and also recognized me, and their smiles (behind their masks) helped raise my spirits.

All three ladies I mentioned helped make what started as a sad day for me, a much better day!

~~~~~~

After Sephora, I went by MAC and finally saw a familiar face! As I neared the store entrance, I looked to see who was working in the store. If I didn't recognize anyone, I'd leave and check again on another visit to the mall. Seeing Linda that day lifted my spirits. She had the same silver-rimmed glasses and straight black hair I remembered from the first time I saw her. She was in the store for the first time since things opened up. It was another positive on a day that sorely needed them, another gift from above to help me through hard times. It was a chance to catch up, let her know about Mom, and find the shade of blue eyeshadow I'd been seeking for a while.

For the next few days, I spent time with my family, making arrangements for Mom's graveside service. By that time, whenever I left the house,

I wore foundation, eyeshadow, lipstick, and dangle earrings. However, my family knew nothing of my transition, which meant toning down everything and removing things I usually wore. When around family, my makeup consisted of tinted moisturizer only, with my original pierced earring studs. I hid all signs of Susannah to avoid unwanted questions.

While the skies were sunny and the weather was warm, I felt more alone than ever... even though I was now around family. I was never one to talk much around them, having very little in common with everyone else. I was the black sheep, the writer who was in the middle of multiple stories while my brothers were successful in technology fields. Less than a year ago, my dad was still commenting on how my long hair would detract from my ability to find work. He was still alluding to how I wasn't behaving the way a man should. I was his oldest child, and his words conveyed how much he viewed me as a failure. I knew who I was, yet it was not the time to truly come out and declare to the world that I never was a man.

During those few days, I saw the patterns of my family's support system. My dad was the center of attention, and rightfully so as he had lost his wife of over fifty years. With Mom in the memory care facility, he'd been at home on his own, though he visited her often and kept busy with different projects on their few acres of land, including the section where he enjoyed farming. With COVID restrictions, he rarely got to see Mom, which was why I was thankful the staff updated him on how she was doing. My brothers also had support: wives, children, and in-laws. They never talked about it, though I suspect they shed many tears with their wives.

Then there was me. I was there alone. My introversion was strong, and I tried to stay out of everyone's way as much as possible. No one asked how I was doing until well after the funeral, and then it was an out-of-the-blue question that felt like it was being asked because it was the polite thing to do. "I'm fine," I said, knowing that would effectively end any follow-up questions. No one knew how hard I was hit by her death.

On the day of the graveside service, less than seventy-two hours after leaving Mom's side for the last time, I was the first to arrive and the last to leave. It felt right since I was Mom's first born and the last to see her alive. When a photo was taken of everyone behind the casket, I stood to one end, slightly off to the side and behind the others—the odd one out. Dad was first to place flowers on her casket. I waited to be last, saying goodbye with tear-filled eyes that no one could see. When everyone left to go back to Dad's place, I stayed and talked with Mom a few minutes, even though her casket was already in the ground and covered. By the time I arrived at his place, the food set out for the remembrance reception was nearly gone. I wasn't hungry, anyway. That day was the last time I'd see most of them for almost a year.

During the last week of August, I made two more trips to Sephora. On the first visit, Betsy told me everyone recognized my comments on the survey. Though it surprised me to find out the associates read the survey comments, the bigger surprise came when Betsy told me the other ladies appreciated what I wrote. Her words were unexpected, and I almost began to cry as I drove home, realizing I had no awareness of making a positive impact in anyone's life. I was like my mom in that respect, for she made a positive impact in the lives of many people and never seemed to know. Once home, the tears flowed as I cried out loud, "I didn't know. I never knew." At that moment, God knew I needed to hear Betsy's words and let the pain I'd felt for so long flow out in those tears.

During that week, I also met Katie in Sephora. She was a brand rep who was an absolute joy to talk with! She was also about my height, a rarity being that I'm around six feet tall. I would marvel at the different ways she styled her long black hair, from simple ponytails to more fancy braids. After helping me find a matte foundation, which was the main item on my list, I mentioned having eyeshadow palettes with colors that would never get worn... at least not on their own. I was clueless what to do with them. At the time, my eyeshadow style was a single shade on my eyelids. I took her to the Fenty palettes and showed her which ones I had at home. The first words out of her mouth were, "Blend them."

What a concept!

If there was a color I wouldn't wear on its own, blend it with other colors that I liked to come up with something new, beautiful, and quite possibly, exciting. And just like that, Katie showed me ways to blend my eyeshadow palettes, opening a door of fashion exploration. The idea that I could blend shades and create new color schemes on my eyes was—you guessed it—eye opening. There was an amazing freedom that settled in with her words, and I was anxious to start playing with colors the next day.

From that conversation with Katie, I experimented with many colors, including the peach palette. While I enjoyed the basic styles of reds, neutrals, and peaches, I soon learned how to become more creative by layering and blending different colors. I did various base shades of the peach or neutral palettes on my eyes, then used shimmery pinks over them to create new rose gold shades. From there, I added blue-greens, lilacs, and even splashy ultraviolet / purple shades. Every time I thought I had a favorite shade, I'd try something new and realize my color options kept growing.

Although August was a painful month with the death of my mom, I also felt a spark of life before the month was over. My transition was in its infancy, yet I seemed to gain momentum after my final visit with Mom. She was the first and only family member to know my truth of being transgender from my own lips. Of my immediate family, only Mom heard me say those words. Although gradual, my world was opening up, and I was slowly coming out of my excruciatingly dark closet.

14

ESSAY: Mom Was My Role Model

My Role Model Is My Mom—And I'm Just Like Her

A Personal Essay by Susannah Dawn

Mom is gone.

It's a recent pain, barely a few weeks old. I was the first of my siblings to be with her, to be held by her. I was her oldest child. I knew and loved her for over half a century. I was the last person to be with her while she was alive, seeing her less than an hour before she passed away.

That in no way diminishes the time my brothers had with her. In reality, I see how each of us was with her for the same amount of time... our entire lives.

During those last precious minutes together, I felt truly blessed to be with her. We were alone in her room with nothing separating us except my mask, a COVID requirement. For me, it was a time to be with my mom and tell her the things I needed to say and needed her to hear. I couldn't have known that visit would be the last time I'd see her alive. While Mom slept, I talked. In my heart, I truly believe she heard every word I spoke that day. My evidence was the way she lifted her head about an inch off her pillow a handful of times as I spoke. To me, it was a sign she knew I was in the room with her and could hear what I said. Most importantly, the visit was a time when I could finally tell her what I wanted—and needed—to say before she left: how much I loved her, how she was the best mom, how sorry I was for not being the best kid, and how glad I was that she was *my* mom. It was also my chance to finally say what I suspected she already knew: I was a trans woman. When I told her, she lifted her head.

Within seventy-two hours, I stood at her graveside service as the "son" my family knew, saying my final goodbyes. It was a small gathering due to COVID restrictions: my father, my brothers and their families, and the pastor. Yet there was some amount of peace to the event. I was the first to arrive and last to leave. During the service, Dad was the first to put a white rose on her casket; I made sure everyone else in attendance went before me. Then I walked by her casket, laid the rose on top and said goodbye with tear-filled eyes.

Something Dad said that afternoon after the service struck a chord and burrowed deep into my thoughts: he didn't know anyone who had a bad word to say about Mom. Thinking about his words, I realized he was right. Mom was one of those rare people whom everyone liked. She brought a special joy and love wherever she went: church, outings with her friends, singing with a choral association, and family gatherings.

When Dad said those words, I realized something else: Mom never knew how much love and joy she brought to others.

I bring this up for a couple of reasons.

First, Dad always commented—and still does—that I'm just like my mom. While there was more truth to that statement than he really knew, the way he said it never felt like a compliment. His words often made me feel I didn't fit in with my family, and that it was easier to withdraw into my closet and stay out of the way.

I was not the strapping, take-charge son he expected. We really had no common interests like he had with my younger brothers. They worked on cars together, while I had no desire to be a mechanic. They went on road trips together, and my brothers developed mannerisms similar to Dad's. My brothers were what Dad expected of his sons: successful, both at work and in their family lives.

Mom was able to flow through her life. She often did things she wanted to do while avoiding many of the things which felt uncomfortable to her. She was soft spoken, rarely raising her voice. She enjoyed watching sports, baking, reading, music, and spending time with her family. I picked up most of these traits, finding enjoyment and relaxation in many of the same things. I also picked up some of her mannerisms, and I often catch myself doing something similar to what Mom would do, be it a gesture, movement, or even singing alone at home.

In my family, Mom was my role model.

Though I never said anything to her while growing up, I knew we were similar as soon as I realized I was really a girl. It was much later before I understood I was a transgender woman. I grew up during the seventies and eighties, when such a concept was not well known. In those decades, anything to do with LGBTQ was viewed negatively. Dad likely thought he'd successfully stamped out what he considered to be repulsive female attributes in me, but in reality, his spankings and verbal comments only taught me to hide my real personality from him. After all Dad did and said to suppress me, I'm amazed I've begun the transition to the woman I've always been.

Mom's wardrobe consisted primarily of skirt outfits, with a few dresses. That was my style, too. I loved the freedom of a good dress and the swish of a beautiful skirt, though originally, I'd only wear such outfits at home. From the start of my transition, Christmas 2019, until just a month after Mom's passing, I only wore jeans, loose t-shirts, sweaters, and sneakers to the mall. Yet at the end of summer, my persona and attire slowly shifted to being more feminine in presentation, even through the jeans, tops, and running shoes.

When I stepped out in leggings and tunics, then dresses in October, the real me was finally stepping out, the girl who was more like her mother every day. I imagine if Mom had seen me wearing those outfits when she was alive, had seen the transformation of my features after even a year of hormones, she would see a daughter who was very much like her in terms of style and dress. She always painted her nails, and that became part of my style, too. Sure, our specific style selections may not have aligned, yet we were both women who loved to wear flowy, feminine outfits.

A second similarity between us began with Mom's strong faith in Jesus, as I have also come to make Him the cornerstone of my foundation.

Mom was the daughter of a Lutheran pastor. She focused on the Lord in everything she did. She played the organ at church during my youth. For most of her life she could be found singing in a choir. Her faith was a joyous aspect of her life, an important feature that not only kept her happy, but was the foundation upon which she always thought about and cared for others. It was much of the reason she was cheerful wherever she went, and why people loved to be around her.

I, too, have my connection with the Lord. Though I am a trans woman, I tried to bring every aspect of my life to the Lord through prayer. I asked for guidance as I moved along the path He placed before me. I let His light shine upon even the darkest places inside, knowing nothing is hidden from Him. With such a focused relationship with my Lord, I became a better person. It was important to me to pray about starting my transition. I believe He opened the door for me to transition and has remained with me as I've continued down my path.

As a youth, I sang in church while Mom played the organ. I enjoyed singing as much as she did, though it became harder for me the further I regressed into my closet. Yet over the past couple years, I found myself singing at home. Sometimes, I can hear Mom's voice in my ear as I sing. At those times, I feel a closeness with her, even though she's gone.

Mom added peace, joy, and love to the lives of others.

She knew how to help people, lift their spirits, and treat others in ways she would want to be treated. Her smile was infectious, making it hard for anyone to be angry around her. She often made time to visit her friends, whether they were in the hospital, at home, or meeting for lunch. She was also a beautiful listener, withholding judgment or interjection when others really needed a friendly ear to bend. In everything she did, she seemed to understand the importance of listening first. She knew the right times to respond, and always spoke with love.

Mom tended to do what she felt was natural. It was why she could genuinely care about others, supporting them through acts of kindness and prayer. She also did her best to not play favorites, making Mom the only person I knew who could genuinely root for both sides of in-state college-rivalry games.

Until Mom passed, I didn't know that like her, I added something positive to the lives of other people. One example was those wonderful ladies at the mall who always treated me kindly. The day after Mom died, I went to the mall to be around the people who had shown me kindness, the ladies at Sephora who only knew me as Susannah. They made the store my safe place. When they saw me, they listened, empathized, and made what was a tough day for me so much better. They gave me the virtual hugs I needed at the time. Though I rarely left comments about store visits, that day I filled out an online survey and mentioned how they truly helped me with more than a simple cosmetic purchase. When I wrote my comments, it was my hope they might see them, though I never believed they would.

I went back a couple days after the funeral to exchange something, and it was then that I learned I made a difference in their lives. The lady who knew me best made a point to thank me for what I wrote. She told me how all the ladies I specifically mentioned in my note truly appreciated my sentiments. Even the store director, who I had not yet met, came up to me, thanking me for what I wrote.

Before that day, I believed that while I tended to gain positive encouragement from others, I couldn't return affirming feelings. I sense Mom may have felt the same way. After learning that what I wrote made such a positive impact on the ladies who were so kind to me, my inner self began to believe I could make other people's days better, just as they did for me.

On that same day, before leaving the mall, I stopped by a favorite fast-food restaurant to get takeout for lunch. It was a place I stopped by frequently, so by that time I recognized some of the staff, even with the mask requirements. There was one lady who often rang up my order. She was kind and would chat briefly, whether there was a line or not. On that day, as I was checking out with my lunch, she told me my entrée was on her! She recognized me and, for some reason I could not quite hear due to the masks, she covered my meal. I was stunned! As I thanked her, she asked my name. When I left, she made a point to say goodbye to me by name.

After that interaction, I understood how being my true self around others brought a positive aspect to their lives, just like Mom. The days after Mom's death were some of the first when I let my true nature out. Thus, as I headed to the mall exit that day, it was difficult to hold back the tears at the revelation that I was becoming a positive impact upon others. Fortunately, the flood gates held until after I got home with my lunch. Once inside the house, however, the tears burst forth as I kept repeating aloud how I never knew I brought anything positive to others. It was a good cry, a cry I had needed for so many years.

Though she's gone, I now understand how a piece of her has always been inside me. Although it had been dormant for so long, it never died nor lost its ability to shine when needed by others. Once I stepped out of the shadows as the woman I've always been, it sparked back to life from its dormant state. It's also why I know a piece of her continues to live inside me, to help me bring joy to those around me, just like Mom.

Dad was right.

I am like Mom and proud to say it.

15

September: a Month of Beginnings

The transition "spark" that originated when I said goodbye to Mom in August began to grow and take hold of me going into September. It was a time when I met Laura, the beauty advisor who was about the same height as me, and had dark hair, full curves, and a perpetually happy demeanor. Like Joy, Laura was critical to my next steps because I asked her a simple question:

"It should be Is there a tear-proof makeup? Since Mom died last month," I said, "I've been crying more than I ever expected. I was the last to see her before she passed away, and the graveside service was less than seventy-two hours after she died."

"You'll want to use 'Aqua Seal' by Make Up For Ever," Laura said. "It's not in the store, though you can get it from Sephora online. I always use it for weddings when I do the makeup." Laura then showed me ways to use it to waterproof my makeup finish, beginning with ways to mix it with my foundation and add it to the setting spray. She then helped me place an order for it to be delivered to my home with free shipping.

I showed her photos of me the weekend of the service and how I looked when I was with my family in "old mode" with just a tinted moisturizer and my original pierced earrings. She said they were good photos, which made my day. To hear someone as experienced with makeup as

Laura tell me that I did well was an amazing, affirming feeling. Then she said something that made my day.

"If it weren't for COVID, I'd give you a hug."

At that point, just hearing her words was as good as getting the hug itself. The last hug I received was from Josie before everything went into shutdown in early March.

Not only did I feel safe in Sephora, I realized the associates in this Sephora were very special, at least in my life. I was amazed how, from the beginning, they accepted and treated me like the person I was inside. I received loving help while learning to use the products and tools available to make me the best-looking lady I could be. I was not used to anyone offering to give me a hug, which added an unexpected layer of friendship in the store. To show my appreciation to everyone in "my" Sephora for all they had done for me in such a difficult time, I wrote a card and gave it to Betsy to share.

~~~~~~

Card given to the Sephora associates on 01 Sep 2021

Since I was unable to provide store-visit comments online after making a purchase on 01 September (even though it was an online purchase through the store), I wanted to write this card of my appreciation—especially as I am a writer / storyteller.

This story stars you, the wonderful staff of the Sephora store. Everyone has been so helpful and open to me when I visit. It seems like a different person assists me on each visit, starting with Joy the day after Christmas last year. And from each of you I have gained a much broader knowledge base of skincare and makeup than I ever expected.

On this visit it was Laura who primarily helped me. I asked her if there was a way to "tear-proof" makeup. The past few weeks have been such an emotional roller coaster with the loss of my Mom, and many tears continue to be shed daily. Laura knew exactly what I needed, showing it to me on the Sephora app and instructing should be instructed me how to use it. Later during this visit, I was helped to purchase it through the store and now anxiously wait for its delivery.

A key part of this story is how your kindness helped an introvert who often feels socially awkward—especially in groups-to feel welcome and accepted. I appreciate how kindhearted you have been to me, and feel that many of you are like the friends and sisters I never had. It has been your wonderful assistance that has helped give me a confidence that I never knew I had.

Thank you.
Susannah Dawn

~~~~~~~~~~~~~~~~~~~~~~~~~~~~~~~~~~~~~

Going into September, my fashion style was limited to jeans, feminine-cut short-sleeve t-shirts, and sneakers. The outfits allowed me to feel like I was being me while androgynously hiding in plain sight. I was slowly stepping out while trying to put aside fears of someone making negative comments about my appearance. Thus, even though I wore differently styled glasses and dangle earrings, it was still difficult to feel I was out as my true self. Although there were certain clothing styles that seemed more proper in terms of how I wanted to present in public, the time was not right to wear them out of the house.

Truth be told, my outfits were no different than what many other women wore walking around the mall and grocery stores. However, to me, wearing more feminine tops, having shoes that were obviously feminine, and ultimately wearing a dress to the mall, were the steps necessary for me to feel I finally stepped out into the world as the woman I have always been inside.

My visits to Sephora were not just improving my makeup and skincare, they helped me overcome many obstacles holding me back from going out as Susannah, my true nature. Whenever I talked with Betsy about this, her comments included, "You need to wear a red dress," and, "Make sure I'm here when you do wear that dress." She never pushed me to go any faster or farther during those early days of transition than I was comfortable, never asked me to take steps that I was not yet ready to take.

To me, Betsy was a true friend. A listener. Supportive. Accepting.

The same type of connection began to occur with other Sephora associates. The more I visited, the more chances there were to speak with new people. It also meant I was opening up and willing to ask them questions. Everything about those visits was part of my learning process, both for cosmetics and skincare, and in talking with other people... socializing. Beauty advisors would come over to me in the store and ask if there was anything they could help me with. My standard answer was still, "I'm fine." The fear of being found out and ridiculed hadn't entirely left, even knowing I was in a safe place. The symptoms of imposter syndrome continued to hold me back.

If I'm being honest with myself, I suspected most of them knew I was a trans woman. I never hid it when I spoke with them, it was noted on the surveys, and I'm sure in the earlier days my voice gave me away. There were some with whom I hadn't talked yet, but who I recognized from January and February, and they no doubt recognized me. My cosmetic skills were still in the early stages. My foundation did not look as polished as I desired, and I wore very basic eyeshadow schemes. I didn't wear mascara, and the concept of putting on eyeliner was totally alien. When taking my mask off at home, the squareness of my face glared at me in the mirror. It screamed at me, saying it was so obvious people would stare at me without the mask. I would remind myself I was only two months into HRT. Even so, in Sephora, no one ever made a remark about my background, commented negatively about my appearance, or looked at me as anything other than a lady looking at cosmetics and skincare products.

As September progressed, I realized most of the associates knew me... by name! There was a point around mid-month when, as I was leaving the store, different associates would say goodbye to me by name. Soon thereafter, I was being greeted by name by beauty advisors as they walked past me to go elsewhere in the store. Many of them I had never spoken with, and yet, they knew me!

There were a couple of key events that occurred during September and early October that impacted me with regards to my fiction writing. In

2019, I entered my first manuscript, "Search for the Armor of God," in the Chanticleer International Book Awards 2019 OZMA Fantasy Book Awards contest. From the end of 2019 through 2020, I watched as my manuscript progressed through the contest: longlist, shortlist, semi-finalist, and finalist. I said prayers of thanks after receiving each successful notice, wondering how far my simple manuscript could progress against published books.

The story itself took a few years to write and develop. It's about an unwanted eldest prince sent by his father on a quest led by his younger brother, who was also the king's heir apparent, to find the legendary Armor of God. It was the first time I'd written a story that long, and I was unsure how it would fare in such a competition. I wrote the entire story before realizing it was too long for one book. Thus, I cut it in half to make it a duology, with the first half reaching finalist status.

The organization that ran the contest held a writing conference in the middle of September. Each day, they unveiled the category and award winners. When winners for the fantasy contest were announced, I learned that my story had placed first in category! Although it did not win the overall award, I was extremely happy. I let my friends know at Sephora, and their excitement for me was heartwarming.

The second event came at the start of October. In June, I submitted a short story, "Command of the Butterfly," to the L. Ron Hubbard's Writers of the Future Contest for science fiction and fantasy. The importance of the submittal was that it was the first story I ever submitted as Susannah Dawn. The story itself was set in the future as a first-person narrative of a trans woman cavalry officer who transitioned while in the military forces. She was the first combat officer to be allowed to do so… and then take a combat cavalry unit command. It was actually the beginning of a larger story about the officer. It was a few days into October when the email arrived informing me the story received an honorable mention, complete with a certificate. The first story submitted as myself received an award, and I received a much-needed confidence boost!

As September progressed, so, too, did my fashion style. The simple t-shirts gave way to cold shoulder tops, tops with a hem twist, and tops with flutter sleeves. My sneakers became black flats. The shades I used for my eyeshadow became more colorful and bolder to the point beauty advisors began to take notice of my eyes and ask how I came up with some of the shades and styles I wore into the store.

Towards the end of the month, I wore a more-feminine blue sweater-top and bone-colored wedges with my jeans. That was a significant departure from my basic look. Though in many ways a simple outfit, my nerves continued to flutter as I walked into the mall, knowing my outfit was a big step out of my closet and into the world. Once in Sephora, Carol was the first person I saw and quickly eased my fears, telling me I looked great! Not only did Carol's support of the outfit make my day, it laid the groundwork towards wearing the style of outfits I've always wanted to wear out of the house. Surprisingly, it only took a few days to take those next steps.

My style reached a new level during the last two visits of the month: leggings, tunics, and booties. On the first visit I wore an oversized orange sweater, black leggings, and one-inch heeled booties. When associates saw me in the store, many commented on how nice my outfit looked. Carol gushed how it was the type of outfit she would absolutely wear. Her words were an affirmation that I was moving in the right direction.

"It's your fault that I wore this look today," I said. "Your support of my outfit last time helped me to finally wear something I've always wanted to wear to the mall."

Carol gladly accepted the responsibility.

The next day I had an errand to run and went by Sephora again. Keeping the leggings, I wore a crimson tunic sweater and three inch black wedge booties. It truly felt like the next step of the natural evolution to be myself in public. Everyone was supportive when they saw me that day, telling me how good I looked or asking where I got the booties. It felt wonderful as I realized how in Sephora, I gained friends I could never have expected even a year ago!

On that last visit, however, I felt awkward leaving the store. I talked with Betsy at the entrance as she was managing the line to enter the store. It was always a positive chat for me. Then I saw three teenage girls at the front of the line looking at me. That's when I became uneasy. It was the first time I actively felt someone staring at me while I was out in public. I had no way to know their thoughts. It's entirely possible they were wondering where I got my outfit or booties. Maybe they just viewed me as a taller lady who managed to find clothing that fit her really well.

It's impossible to know what someone is thinking, especially when half their face is covered, so it was easy for fear to control my thoughts and fill in any blanks. When I realized they were all looking at me, I wondered if they were also talking amongst themselves about me. I worried they might actually view me as trans, thereby allowing my imposter syndrome to take root. Inside, I started to panic and needed to get out of the mall as fast as possible. Although I was able to remain calm, knowing Betsy was there and had my back if anyone said anything, once I was out of the mall, I went straight home wondering if that feeling would ever subside. Would it ever decrease to the point where I could grow more as myself, or would the fear of being seen as an imposter push me back into the darkness of a forbidding closet?

October was about to give me the answer.

16

First the Skirt... Then the Dress

Susannah was coming out of the closet at a pace that far exceeded anything I could have imagined or ever thought possible. I went out in public wearing almost anything that felt right and comfortable, which amazed me. As I walked amongst the other people at the mall, I still looked around, trying to see if they saw through my makeup and outfits. Other times, my tunnel vision reemerged to keep me from paying attention to anyone else lest I see them staring. I knew I was very good at being myself, Susannah, yet still had a lack of confidence from imposter syndrome. My feelings that others could see right through my façade kept me from wearing the outfits I had always wanted to wear.

I understood I could walk into a room as myself, Susannah, and no one was likely to question my authenticity as a woman. Yet my fear was strong; it waited for someone to misgender me, to stand up and say I was a fake. I knew I was a woman and have known it all my life. However, having to live as someone I was not, with the wrong hormones coursing through my body, also left marks that I needed to overcome. Spending a half century acting like the gender of my exterior had created mannerisms and styles that required time to undo. Simple things like walking involved concentration to make sure my center of movement was between my hips instead of my chest, while simultaneously observing the length and pace of my strides. I was a trans woman, standing up in life in such a way that anyone who didn't know me wouldn't see me as anyone other than woman. All the while, fear told me I was an imposter and searched for proof that others saw it, too.

As I struggled with overcoming my fears and learned mannerisms, I soaked in everything I could about skincare and cosmetics at Sephora. I took to the subjects like a fish takes to water. My cosmetics skills had improved, especially over the past two months. I wasn't afraid to ask skincare questions and saw that my own skincare routine was paying off. I wore clothing that felt appropriate to my gender, then slowly developed and expanded into styles that felt more like me.

My wardrobe expansion was the most significant thing to happen in October. I still felt trepidation as I stepped out of my car into stores. I worried about how others viewed me. I was thankful for the masks, just not for the reason most people would expect. The masks boosted my confidence around being seen in public as a woman. When all anyone could see were my eyes, glasses, earrings, and hair, it seemed less likely they would misgender me. Masks, especially the ones I had with flowers and cute colorful designs, helped me feel more at ease to shop for what I needed, and be myself.

On a Tuesday in October, I left the house wearing a skirt for the first time! It was a knee-length denim skirt which I dressed up with a red blouse decorated with small ruffles, nude nylons, and black two and three-quarter inch heels. It was a significant departure from what I usually wore. While I knew I had positive support once I got to the mall, my first stop was the grocery store, a place where I knew no one.

My nerves went into overdrive once I parked. I wore sneakers for driving and replaced them with my heels before getting out of the car. I became self-conscious as I opened the door and stepped out into the parking lot. Even though I found walking in heels came fairly natural to me, I practiced at home where the floors were carpeted. I took each step across the pavement carefully, intentionally. I tried to focus on my pace on the hard surfaces instead of looking around to see if anyone was staring at me. It was slightly overcast with a cool chill in the air, and it felt amazing as it kissed my legs. Although I wanted to enjoy the sensation longer, it was more important to concentrate on each step as I approached the entrance. I had no desire to fall. By ignoring the fears, a sense of invigoration flowed through me as I was finally out in public wearing an outfit I'd wanted to wear since high school. The only description I could think of was a sense of pure joy. After completing my purchase and returning to my car, it dawned on me that most people in the store paid no attention to me. Those who did notice me were very casual, seeing me as any other shopper when we crossed paths in the various grocery aisles.

My confidence moved up a notch by the time I entered the mall. My first stop was MAC, where both Linda and Lori said I looked really good. Their comforting words put me more at ease.

When Linda asked if I was nervous, I said, "There's definitely a fear in the back of my mind that people will watch, or even stare at me. There was a man sitting on a bench outside the store who seemed to be doing just that, which concerned me, although it looks like he's gone, now."

Linda and Lori were always supportive of me. The MAC shop is part of a larger department store, and the handful of ladies I met there became friends. Each played a role in my transformation. Linda was there from the beginning, helping me pick out my first lipstick the day after Christmas, which was beginning to feel like a long time ago. Lori has been a little sparkplug for me, always interested in seeing what I'd done with my makeup or giving feedback on my outfits. Whenever Lori commented about what I wore, I knew it was a good choice. If there was no comment, then I'd either dressed like any other woman in the mall, or I'd worn the outfit before, so it didn't make much of an impression.

What I realized that day was how my lipstick color choices had naturally evolved. At the time, the only lipsticks I had were MAC. The first shades before March were as close to my natural color as possible while still visibly showing I was wearing lipstick. Going into the stay-at-home period, I started to expand into some darker shades of red. Once familiar faces were back in the store, I began to look at even darker and brighter reds along with colorful pinks for my lips. Just like the great associates at Sephora, Linda and Lori put me at ease to go beyond my comfort zone in color choices.

Sephora was my next stop, and it was one of the few times the person at the door didn't recognize me, asking if I'd been in since they reopened.

In fact, of the ladies I usually talked with in Sephora, only Carol was there. Yet talking with her was a huge boost to overcoming my doubts about how I looked in public.

"It's the first time I've worn a skirt in public," I told her.

"You look great," she said, "and I really like where you're headed. Your shoes are nice. Are they new?"

"I've probably had them for six or eight years," I replied. "This is the first time they've been out of the house, and this is the longest I've worn heels... I'm starting to feel them."

"I really wish they'd let us do makeup applications," Carol said, "as I'd love to do your makeup!"

Makeup applications were some of the personal services provided by Sephora. A beauty advisor would clean all existing make-up off the customer's face then do a full makeover. These applications were more involved than the simple foundation shade matching Joy did for me that first day. The pandemic and health concerns, however, had eliminated personal services and the opportunity to try samples in store. Color matching was done using small clear plastic palettes. The product went on the palette and was held up to the face to match.

Other associates had expressed the same wish as Carol. It surprised me how many would say those same words. Every time, I felt surrounded by good friends, or even big sisters who couldn't wait to help a younger girl with her makeup. Carol had previously shared some eyeshadow tips, suggesting I start on the outside of my eyes. It would allow for a lighter amount of the color on the inside of my lids and open up my eyes. My visit was a chance to show her how I tried to put her advice into practice. "I like it," she said.

In Sephora, I found it important to listen to what each associate said as they answered my questions. I tried to be as honest and open as possible because, let's face it, they had a whole lot more experience in skincare and cosmetics than I did! I always tried what they suggested. If it didn't work, I could return a product, or not spend time trying makeup tricks that weren't right for me. When it did work, the results were usually amazing. Whether new eyeshadow styles, moisturizers, or great makeup cleaners, everything they showed me significantly improved my skills.

That same day, I learned more people in the mall knew who I was than I realized. When I went to my usual fast-food restaurant in the food court, one of the servers was especially kind as she put together my selections. I always included her by name when filling out the online surveys. It didn't hurt that each completed survey provided a code for one free entrée if I purchased two. On that day she wasn't there, however, someone who looked like the manager said something to the cashier before I paid for my meal.

The cashier said, "Thank you for your survey comments. We really appreciate them."

"Thank you," I said, surprised at his words. I also saw that he gave me a free cookie with my meal.

As I left the mall to go home, I wondered how many people truly recognized me, even if they never talked with me. I felt fortunate God had put good people on my path, people who helped me to feel comfortable being myself. When I'm living life as my true self—Susannah—despite the fears trying to control me, I still feel more genuine and positive around people. It's a feeling of letting the Spirit flow through me. I only want to bring positive energy wherever I go.

Having survived my first day in a skirt, I filled the next couple of days contemplating the next logical step in going out as I'd always viewed myself. I prepared for the biggest move yet in my transition: wearing a dress to the mall. My goal was to wear a knee-length red sweater dress to Sephora. As I got dressed and went to my car, a variety of emotions ebbed and flowed through me. I was excited to finally wear a cute dress outside the home, to truly feel free as myself. While I loved the skirt and blouse I'd worn earlier, there was still a slight constraint as the waist of the skirt could, at times, feel tight, a sensation that didn't occur with the dress. Thus, for me, wearing a dress and nylons was the epitome of being feminine, of being myself, and of feeling freedom as a woman. I tried to push the fears of what others might think away as I slipped on my bone-colored wedges and went to my car.

At the mall, I anxiously walked to the entrance. Inside, I headed for my first stop: Amazon. It was easier to return items to the Amazon store in the mall than to pack them. Walking through the mall, I was self-conscious with each step. I kept glancing at my reflection in the darker windows as I walked past stores, making sure I looked alright. I was glad to have chosen the wedges; the two-inch heels were much easier to walk in than the pumps I wore with the skirt. The return went smoothly inside Amazon, and by the time I was back in the hallway, I hadn't noticed anyone looking at me oddly, nor did I hear any negative comments.

I was doing fine until I entered Macy's. One of my goals for that trip was to go shoe shopping, which I felt would be easier in a dress. Unfortunately, when I got about a third of the way into the store towards the shoe department, I saw a lot of sales ladies chatting in the aisles of the cosmetics area. Realizing I'd have to pass by so many women in a narrow corridor worried me. It was possible they might ask questions as I headed towards the shoes, and I wasn't ready to interact with so many strangers. I turned around and went to MAC instead.

There, I was safe with Linda and Evelyn. They were surprised to see me in the dress—which actually felt good to hear. They both said I looked great, and that red was a good color for me. I wasn't used to hearing such positive, affirming words from others, and it felt wonderful to hear their comments. My worries about presentation were able to abate a bit, especially as I felt the honesty of their words.

"How are you doing, being out in a dress?" they asked.

"It feels good," I said. "I tried to focus on two thoughts when I left the house today. The first was on who I would see at the mall, knowing how many of you (including the ladies at Sephora) have been so supportive of me. Second, I tried to focus on not thinking about the details of what I was doing... just leave the house dressed in the outfit I wanted to wear, and go shopping."

When Linda left to work on a project, it was my first real chance to talk with Evelyn. The store was quiet. We started off with my questions about tinted moisturizer and a couple of other products. Then I told her how I became anxious when headed to the women's shoes in the Macy's store. Even though I had friends in MAC, it was a small store with the one side totally exposed to everyone walking through the mall, and I still felt more exposed to the public's eye than when inside the Sephora store. Evelyn asked if she could introduce me to one of Macy's personal shoppers.

When she mentioned that the lady could pick things out for me to try on, I replied that what I really wanted was to be able to go shoe shopping myself yet have someone with me for support.

Our conversation was a little more personal with each other that day. We had a lot of similarities regarding fashion, even with the definite age and height differences between us. We both preferred having clothing with a high waist: pants, leggings, etc. Neither of us was afraid to wear pantyhose, especially as they enhance the look of the legs. Evelyn was surprised I only started to come out after Christmas, and that most of my cosmetics skills had only occurred during the past six weeks.

When I left MAC, I made a beeline for Sephora. While the day had gone well so far, it was there where I hoped to truly feel at ease. Sephora was my safe place, someplace to be my true self, yet until that point, I hadn't worn a dress there. Even with Linda and Evelyn's positive feedback, I still needed to know what my friends at Sephora thought. Walking through the halls and around the people milling about, my emotions fluctuated between the excitement of entering the store in a dress for the first time, and fear something might go wrong either on my way there or after I entered.

Nearing the main door, I saw Betsy was the greeter. Her excitement at seeing me in the red dress was amazing! She wanted to give me a hug right there—though COVID kind of nixed that possibility. Then she told me I really made her happy! Betsy was my biggest supporter to wear a dress and was adamant it had to happen when I was ready. She never pushed me to do anything before I was willing, but she was resolute that the first dress had to be red... and I had to come when she was at the store.

As we talked at the entrance, I showed her a photo of the skirt and top I wore a couple days earlier. She was obviously bummed to have missed seeing me that day. Since there was no line at the entrance, I had a chance to pitch a book idea I had about my growth and the critical role that Sephora played in my transition.

Entering the store, Betsy said they were having a Charlotte Tilbury (CT) event. That meant the Charlotte regional account executive, Elle, was there to answer product questions, and they had various specials and gifts available for customers based on the amount of CT products they purchased. When I saw Elle, I really wanted to talk with her, both about the CT brand and because she looked like a great person. However, I became extremely self-conscious. Elle was more "fashionable" across the board than me, which played a part in the concerns holding me back. Then there was the question of what to say if we did talk. I became voice conscious and decided to avoid talking with anyone unless I had already talked with them during other visits.

I felt that Elle was watching me at various times in the store. Hindsight says she'd be looking at everyone to see who might need some assistance. Still, I worried she might "see through me." Fortunately, I was talking with Betsy when I first noticed Elle, which helped lessen that fear from the start.

I was astonished at how many of the ladies in Sephora noticed I was wearing the dress and came over to comment and tell me how good I looked. Brenda was one of the first to see me enter the store. She quickly came to say I looked nice. Later, Sally came out of nowhere to say how great I looked! After checking out, I thought I saw Wendy and went looking for her. She was also excited to see me in the dress, telling me the color looked good on me.

Most of the comments came from the associates who knew me. It was possible many realized it was the first time I'd worn a dress in public. Throughout the start of my journey, their words of support and encouragement have been one of the greatest blessings to me. And while I'd only been a regular visitor for two short months, there was a feeling of being accepted and slowly becoming a part of their community every time I stepped into Sephora. On the more technical side, they helped me improve my understanding of skincare and cosmetics, and I would also learn about haircare, which I desperately needed.

Actual Sephora survey comments from store visit the day I wore a dress for the first time:

On this particular day, I was nervous when I left my home—it was my first time out of the house wearing a dress. When I arrived at Sephora... I was overwhelmed by the joy I was greeted with... many of those fears were removed, and the day was made more special than I expected. Each associate who knows me made a point to come over to me and compliment me on my outfit, and I could see their smiles behind their masks.

As I spoke with some of the associates I know from previous visits, I asked about my makeup to get their opinions on how I did, seeking ways to improve. When they noted that my eyeliner looked great, I thanked them and said that I've only used eyeliner for less than two weeks—before that, I had never used it because it seemed difficult to put on. The responses were heartfelt and amazing when they realized how fast I've learned new makeup techniques.

~~~~~~~~~~~~~~~~~~~~~~~~~~~~~~~~~~~~~

Proper hair care was foreign to me. My hair looked rough, at least in my eyes. Although it was below my shoulders when I first met Joy, it had grown down to my chest by October. While I loved my long hair, I needed help to learn how to properly take care of it, along with my scalp. It had never been styled beyond leaving it long and loose, or tying it up in a ponytail. Plus, it was over three years since my last haircut, although I did get a simple trim Christmas Eve to make sure the ends were in good shape.

Enter Sally. She was about five feet tall with blonde hair, blue eyes, and ample energy. She was always ready to answer questions. Everyone in the store pointed me towards her when I asked about hair care, and I quickly left my hair's health in her capable hands. Right off the bat, Sally connected me with a shampoo to try for the scalp itching I'd experienced. Soon my head was feeling better. I looked to her as my hair-care expert.

That was the beginning of a hair-health routine that remained in her hands until she left the store. As I considered possible hair styles and color options, I wouldn't make a move without talking with her first. Sally's knowledge provided me with a feeling of security. Having enjoyed watching my hair grow over the past few years, it was important to be sure I didn't make mistakes that could damage it. I fully trusted Sally.

I purchased a number of products as I acquired knowledge of cosmetics, skincare, and haircare. I began thinking about finding ways to save and possible payment options. That led me to a new chapter in my Sephora experience.

17

Sephora Visa!!!

In October, I decided to apply for the Sephora credit card. There were perks that made sense when thinking about products I'd recently purchased, my wish list, and my recurring purchases such as hair care items, moisturizers, and foundation. The points benefits and special sales for different Beauty Insider levels made getting the card seem sensible. While building my makeup and skincare collection, the rebate points provided by the card—along with the periodic discounts—would help to reduce some costs down the road.

Thus, by the middle of October, I decided to sign up for the card, unaware of the bonuses I'd experience during the process. The first bonus was finally having the excuse to talk with three associates I'd wanted to meet since before the shutdown: Marie, Deborah, and Brian.

The process kicked off while talking with Wendy. After mentioning how I was thinking about signing up for the Sephora card, her blue eyes sparkled as she jumped at the idea and said she could help with the process. We went to the register area where Marie helped me fill out the quick online application. While I recently changed my Sephora Beauty Insider account to my preferred name, I knew my legal name was required for the card. I completed and submitted the form, and the answer to my application came soon after: authorized!

While excited about the new card, I was also hoping to get my preferred name on it. I asked Wendy and Marie about it. Wendy went to get someone to assist, returning with Deborah. I finally got to talk with her!

"Have you legally changed your name?" Deborah asked. She was as tall as me, fairly thin, with long, straight, brown hair.

"No," I replied. "While I understood the need for the legal name to get and use the card, I was hoping it would be possible to put a preferred name on the card."

"I don't see why not," she said. "I suggest you call the customer service after the card's approval, and ask them to do that."

As I thanked her, Marie wrote down the phone number for me to call.

I remembered seeing Marie at the registers before the shutdown. She was my height, always smiling, and her dark eyes were bright while her black hair was smooth and very long. I wanted to talk with her since then. Being an introvert, however, I had no idea how to start a conversation with her. I always hoped the chance would occur to check out with her at the cashier station, thinking that would open the door to talk. It never happened. It was after the card approval, when she commented that she really liked my nail color, that we began to talk. When I told her the color, inside I was overjoyed to finally speak with her.

The next morning, I called the Sephora credit card company to see about putting my preferred name on the new card. The representative I spoke with said he was able to help me out with that. After we talked a few minutes, he put me on hold to confer with his supervisor. When he returned, he called me "Mrs!" He said I should have the card in the next week to ten days and told me my preferred name would be on it. I was so excited to have my first credit card with my preferred name. That was bonus number two.

When I applied for the card, I wasn't totally sure if I was approved for the store card or visa card. It was a couple days later when I realized it was a real visa card. Not only was it truly my first credit card as Susannah, it gave me the freedom to use it anywhere and not worry about people trying to match my face with the name on the card; the two aligned perfectly. My new face was on a new card!! A third bonus!

Though that may seem like the end of the story, what happened next made life a bit more complicated. Almost two weeks after the phone call with customer service, my new card hadn't arrived. I was anxious to get it, so I called the credit card company. Somehow during the conversation, the person on the phone cancelled the card that was somewhere in the mail and issued a new card.

I stopped by my Sephora store later that day and told Marie what happened.

"I want to call them right now and make them fix the problem!" she said to me. At that moment, even though I'm probably old enough to be her parent, Marie felt like a big sister looking out for me. It felt good knowing that someone cared enough about me to want to help.

During my checkout process, I talked with Brian for the first time, having recognized him from before the shutdown. He called the credit card customer support for me about my card before ringing up my purchase at the register.

To continue complicating matters, my original card showed up early the next week, yet it was no longer valid due to the new card being in the mail. My wait time was extended, which was difficult. However, I forced myself to not call the credit card company to check on the status. My fear was, if I called them for any reason, they might cancel that card and reissue it again, thereby delaying the delivery that much longer. I was excited to get my new card, and helpless to do anything except wait, and wait, and wait.

It must have seemed like an odd melodrama to the associates in Sephora. There I was, anxious to get my new card with my preferred name on it, a further validation of my true self. The few associates who knew both me and the situation, tended to check in on me to make sure I was doing alright during the waiting period. A couple truly felt like they empathized with me, which was a blessing and helped calm me down.

I don't remember ever being as excited for a credit card as I was when it finally showed up. The envelope was addressed to my preferred name, and all I could do was thank God for allowing me to have this new card with my name on it. I felt more empowered to go out as Susannah and make purchases without the fear of being questioned when my face didn't match the name on the credit card. With my new card in hand, I headed to Sephora to let them know it was finally here!

There were only a few associates that I showed the card to, including Betsy, Deborah, Marie, Wendy, and Brian. My Sephora card was another important step in my transition and a major step towards freedom!

18

The "Blame Game" ;-)

I was astounded at the extent my skills grew in just a couple short months. Though no expert, my abilities to use new products genuinely took off. On top of that, because I actively expanded myself in terms of talking with different Sephora beauty advisors, I learned new skills and tricks from different people. That, in turn, led me to start keeping track of which Sephora associates were "responsible" for different aspects of my growth and transition. That included identifying who might be the most responsible—the most helpful—in guiding me in specific aspects of skincare and makeup skills. Thus, if someone said the Fenty Peach palette shades of eyeshadow I was wearing looked good on me, I could say, "It's Katie's fault I now have the Fenty peach palette, as I'd never have selected it without her encouragement. She said it would bring out my eyes." So, though it may sound like I was blaming someone for something, it was my way of crediting where credit was due for my growth.

At the beginning of my transition, Laura was the first to tell me Aqua Seal could waterproof my foundation before I applied it. With Mom's recent passing, I was tired of having my makeup run when I started crying, which often occurred out of the blue. Not only did Laura show me how to use the drops with my foundation, but she also recommended adding drops into my setting spray to give an overall waterproof set to my makeup.

It was Katie who recommend blending eyeshadow colors, especially if they were colors I didn't expect to wear on their own. It was amazing how many new colors were "added" to my palettes without the need to buy more. She also recommended the Fenty Peach eyeshadow palette, which had gold / orangish colors. Originally, when I saw it, they seemed the wrong shades for me. However, I trusted her when she said they'd make my blue eyes stand out. My trust was rewarded with more great color options, eventually including some beautiful rose golds.

In addition to improving my hair care routine, Sally taught me how to use my fist as a makeup palette. Every time she showed me samples, she used the back of her hand, blending the cosmetics before applying them. She also introduced me to lips stains, suggesting I blend them if one shade seemed too dark or too light... or if I just wanted to be creative and make new colors. Sally's biggest impact on me was being the root reason I love—adore—sparkles... especially in and on my eyeshadow! Before Sally, the idea of sparkles was foreign to me. Then, with her suggestion of using Urban Decay's "Space Cowboy" as an eyeshadow topper, Sally opened up a whole new world for me!

In some ways, Wendy was a sister, mother, and friend all rolled into one. After mentioning to her how I was having difficulty getting into my end-of-day cleaning routine, she gave me some sage—and blunt—advice: "Don't remove your bra until you remove all of your makeup and moisturize your face." It was clear, simple, and showed how much she accepted me. She was also one of the people who helped me design a skincare routine that significantly improved the smooth youthful appearance of my face.

Carol was involved with several firsts, starting with concealer. From there, she helped me select my first eyeliner, providing the quick and simple guidance I needed to begin to understand the many ways to use it. She also gave me tips on makeup application and design, especially for my eyeshadow.

Lynda became critical to my skincare routine. One of her best qualities was how she was always straightforward. She was one of the first people to help me realize that, now that I was on HRT, my hormones would affect—and possibly change—my skin type and texture. When I realized I no longer had combination / oily skin, she already knew it, telling me she'd never seen the telltale shine on my face.

Cara helped find skincare products and showed me the best ways to apply them. She had an Irish accent and red hair. Cara taught me to place serums under my eyes, starting closer to my nose and rubbing them towards the outer edge of my eyes since that's how those areas drained. As my skin began to become drier from the hormones, she helped find the right, cost-effective products to help add and sustain moisture, thereby improve my complexion for the application of my makeup.

When I mentioned being unhappy with the finish of my foundation, Julie finally explained how to use a wet sponge in a way that sounded as simple as it turned out to be. Slightly shorter than me, she had dark hair that fell below her shoulders and was a wizard when it came to eye shadow looks. An energetic lady, she taught me how to provide the smoother, more-uniform appearance for my foundations that I'd been lacking.

Brenda was someone I could count on for advice across the spectrum. She was also the beauty advisor I'd known the longest. At the start, during January and February, she was usually the one I'd ask about Joy. She helped me many times, beginning in those early days with a cleanser and overnight moisturizer. After the reopening, I often went to Brenda with questions on new eyeliner colors, blushes, eyeshadow, and foundation... pretty much anything that crossed my mind. She was always cheerful and happy to help me find new products.

While most of my lipsticks were from MAC, Heather saw me in the Make Up For Ever section and came over to talk. She highly recommended their holiday sparkle lipsticks. I told her I already had plenty of lipsticks between MAC and a Sephora lip stain set I'd recently bought thanks to Sally. Heather had long, bright-blonde hair, was slightly shorter than me, was always cheerful to talk with, and turned out to be very persuasive. While I was initially able to hold off, the seed was planted. Between Christmas and New Year's Day, when those lipsticks went on an additional discount, I ended up buying all five!

I wanted something to help keep my hands so they wouldn't age and weather like my mom's hands. While I'd talked with a few associates about moisturizing options, when I mentioned it to Elle with Charlotte Tilbury, she brought me over to a new Kiehl's product that just came out in the store: Milk-Peel toner. It was exactly what I was seeking. It was also another example of finding a product sold for a specific application, in that case for the face, that worked perfectly for something else.

I started progressing towards more colorful eyeshadow looks in October, which made it difficult to pull back to the natural looks I wore pre-pandemic. With a family event scheduled for June 2021, I knew I needed to go with a minimal finish on my eyes. It would be the first time I saw them in almost a year, and eyeshadow had become a staple of my morning routine. Since my family didn't know about my transitioning, it was important to look as much like I did at my mom's funeral as possible. Coming out to them was not yet on my mind. Marie provided a great idea by suggesting the use of a light neutral shadow topped off with a champagne finish. When I tried that, it was just the "wearing makeup yet can't obviously tell it's makeup" look I was desperately seeking!

A wonderful aspect of my friends at Sephora was that they taught me things that helped me be the authentic me, yet were not necessarily make-up or skincare focused. Case in point: boots. I always wondered where Cheyenne got her boots as I thought she had the best—and often cutest—boots I'd seen. I recognized her from before the shutdown. She was a little shorter than me with dark brown hair and a consistent smile. When I finally got up the courage to talk with her in November to ask about her boots, she told me her source. I checked the website that night. That was the moment I realized I was a boot girl! From that first order of black over-the-knee boots along with a pair of black, three inch block-heel ankle booties, I've enjoyed expanding that part of my wardrobe. It was a total surprise when other women stopped me in stores to compliment me on my boots! It felt validating when they spoke up unexpectedly to let me know I made a great fashion choice.

While many ladies were supportive as I expanded my "public" wardrobe, Carol's support held the largest sway. She laid the groundwork for each of my major wardrobe steps over a short three-week period between September and October. When she said I looked great in a blue feminine sweater, I found confidence to try leggings and tunics. When she said one of those outfits was something she'd wear, I stepped up to wear a skirt. Her positive words about that outfit led me to take the biggest step—one I never thought I'd take in my lifetime: I wore the red dress to the store! Had anyone told me even six weeks earlier when I was stepping out of my closet in trepidation that I'd soon be wearing a dress to Sephora, I'd have said, "No way."

In a conversation with Wendy, she recommended getting a steamer to help remove wrinkles from clothes that are more difficult to iron. It came up when I wore a new black steampunk layered skirt. While I tried to iron it, many of the wrinkles within the various layers of black material refused to disappear. Wendy said a good, small, handheld steamer would remove most wrinkles that are hard to remove with an iron. I found an inexpensive and well-rated steamer online. Though it could take a bit longer than ironing, the results were significantly better. Wendy helped me improve the look of my wardrobe, and I'm so grateful for her advice!

Betsy helped me to let go of my difficulties in making friends and my inability to trust people. I could always be up front with her about how I was doing and where I hoped my transition would lead. If I mentioned having some emotional difficulties, she always checked in to make sure I was doing alright and to let me know she was there for me. Betsy was the first to let me know it was alright to open up when I was ready.

And then there was Joy, who was extremely important as she was there for me that first day. Because of her genuine kindness, never pushing and always encouraging, she helped me finally move forward. Joy made it possible for me to take my first steps out of a dark closet where I felt banished most of my life and enter the light of being my true self. Joy helped this girl begin to fly!

Most of all, everyone at Sephora, in one way or another, encouraged me to experiment with makeup and seek my own cosmetic artistic style. Creativity is part of my core. I'm always looking for ways to explore new ideas and stories. In Sephora, that guided how I learned my own feminine style.

Using my own words, "It was Sephora's fault that I was able to gain confidence and grow, to transition into the person I've always been." Sephora provided a safe place to walk, talk, explore, be creative, and make real friends.

19

ESSAY: Through Transition I Regained My Freedom

Through Transition I Regained My Freedom

A Personal Essay by Susannah Dawn

In my earliest years I was carefree, vivacious, and open. Upon entering elementary school, I made friends with ease. Even my aunt noted how bouncy and happy I was back then. At her wedding, around age six, people literally put their hands on my shoulders to keep me still when photos were taken. During those years, I felt free and unjudged; the world was open and allowed me to be myself.

By age three I knew I was a girl. When I started to exhibit my female self around age seven, the abuse I received pushed the vibrant person I was at heart into a deep dark closet. It was the start of my slide towards introversion. I found it difficult to feel safe around people. The ability to open up and make friends melted away for fear of being hurt. Abuse and fear led me to withdraw from the world, and it's just now, almost a half century later, that I'm coming out to regain my lost sense of freedom.

There are many ways for a person to be abused. Some forms are mistakenly viewed as worse than others, and I am thankful what happened to me was not as bad as it could have been. However verbal abuse and phys-ical actions towards me still resulted in varying degrees of scarring. The worst part of being abused, for me as a victim, was how it wasn't always obvious. Often the abuser's focus was to cause shame, to control me with the goal of achieving some form of desired change. Yes, "shaming" of any kind is a form of abuse. It puts the abuser in a position of superiority to intimidate, and force change that aligns with the abuser's purposes. It's designed to tear down the victim, even if they did nothing wrong.

My confusion about who I was first got me into trouble when I tried to express my inner self instead of conforming to my outer physique. Know-ing I was a girl, I tried on my mother's clothes. I'm unsure how often it happened before my father caught me. However, when he did, that was when the carefree person I was shrank into the closet, slowly closing the door on my true nature and letting the quiet introvert emerge. My father spanked me every time he caught me, undoubtedly thinking his actions would cause me to stop such "foolish" activities. Fortunately, the spank-ings did not last long as I became good at hiding my true self from my parents.

However, though the spankings subsided, my father had more meth-ods in his arsenal to "set me right." There were numerous times he took to teasing and ridiculing me when I did something that could be interpret-ed as girlish. During my youth, girls played with dolls while boys played with action figures. "Big Jim" was one of the series of toys for boys, and I wanted the Big Jim Sports Camper. To my delight, my parents gave it to me for Christmas one year. However, whenever I played with it, my dad often made comments about how I was playing with dolls, making it sound like a bad thing for a "boy" to do. I had other action figures over the years, and all were accompanied by the memories of how he teased me, always with a silly smile on his face—sometimes laughing as he did it. He never knew a deep pain grew inside me, and that his behaviors made me feel unimportant. Although deep down I knew my parents loved me, I felt no love in those moments, and so continued to close myself off from them for self-preservation, to keep my inner self safe.

When we were alone, my mom often gave excuses for my father's behavior. Sometimes she said he was "just trying to be funny," or that he never got along with his father, which implied he didn't have a good role model for fatherhood. She would say he really did love me. However, her comments couldn't heal my hurt heart because his words and actions didn't stop. Unfortunately, my mom's attempts at excuses only put her on his side of my pain.

There were other ways my father's comments whittled away at who I was. Whenever he saw me wearing my pants at or above my waist, he said they were too high and to pull them down. It was obvious to me that my pants belonged at my waist, especially as the inseam length was proper—I never went out with my pants looking like they were high-water pants. Dad also refused to let my hair get any longer than what he deemed appropriate, implying longer hair belonged to girls. Since he was the only one to cut my hair, he controlled the result of each haircut—which was never even close to the length I wanted. Then there were the times he told me I should work out and build up muscle, suggesting that to be a proper "man" I should be strong and burly. From an early age, I had no desire to be "muscle bound" and often said so. The idea of building up muscles felt wrong.

The teasing crossed over from home to school when I was in second or third grade. I had to carry my books and school supplies in paper bags from the grocery store. To make sure the bags didn't break, I carried them in front of me with both arms. We lived in the countryside, outside a small town. Only one school bus route passed our home, and all the K-12 students rode the same bus. Some of the students, especially the older ones, began to call me "Cinderella." I had no idea why they were so mean until one of the girls my age said it was because I carried my bag like a girl. Although the girl in me didn't really mind the name, being teased wasn't fun. I found a new way to carry the bags, rolling the top down to make a handle, which made them more difficult to carry. And yet, even though I made the change, the name calling continued until we moved.

By middle school, I felt the safest thing to do was keep to myself, which meant having no friends to hang out with. Those were the years when I was physically bullied. I never mentioned it to my parents because, well, since my father already teased me, why should I expect his sympathy or support? All I could do was put up with it. With no friends and a bully who kept bothering me, I was truly on my own. One day during the second year of middle school, I had enough from the bully. When he started to bother me, I threw my books on the ground and chased him across the school yard. I never caught him and have no idea what I would have done if I had. However, it gave me a few months' relief from his antics before he began to bully me again. I can only guess I was his target because I was always alone with no one to support me.

Besides school-related issues, there were other events during those years that pushed me deeper into the closet. Each one increased the distance between me and my classmates until I felt safest staying away from other students and group situations. Being alone was safer than the pain of exposing myself to hurtful words, whether they were intentional or not.

In middle school, my mom drove me daily to a week-long summer basketball camp. I believed there was nothing special about my skills as coaches and other kids never seemed to notice me. But somehow, during one of the last games before the end of camp, I scored twenty or more points. Since I never made more than one or two baskets in a game, it surprised me. Personally, it felt good to succeed at something, even if no one else said anything about it. During the awards ceremony on the last day of camp, I didn't expect to get anything as it was rare for me to receive positive recognition. Thus, when the coach started talking about the most improved player award, I thought nothing of it... until some of the guys behind me whispered loud enough for me to hear that they hoped I didn't receive it. The award went to someone else. What I didn't realize at the time was how commonplace that type of the verbal attack was to me at such a young age. I only knew such comments were further proof I should not to try to make friends, since it was obvious no one liked me, though I had no idea why.

Even after moving cross country before high school, I was still unable to make friends. My first year in the new school, a classmate decided to make me his personal verbal punching bag. Any time he could humiliate me for laughs, he would. When the teacher of the health class said we could safely write down any question we had about the current subject—reproduction, and that she would openly answer it without identifying the student, I believed her. I had arrived at the school halfway through the topic, so I really didn't understand it. When she read my question, the classmate sitting next to me made a point to insure everyone knew the "stupid question" was mine. The teacher said nothing to defend me and ignored my question altogether. The teasing pushed me further into my closet, keeping me away from interactions with classmates due to the fear of even more teasing.

My childhood made it difficult for me to trust people as an adult. Trust is a basic element of friendship. I did manage to find trust with two people—two marriages, though the first was another example of opening up my heart only to have it hurt and tossed out.

My first marriage had rough patches before she ultimately chose to divorce me. Before our divorce, on a visit to my in-laws, my mother-in-law and I drove alone to the store. My wife and I were in a bad place, and I honestly answered some of her questions. Unfortunately, the conversation did not remain between the two of us. On the three-hour drive home from the in-laws, I was grilled about things I said to my mother-in-law, and then questioned about my reasons for saying what I did. My ex also told me to go to counseling to "get fixed," since I was obviously the problem in the relationship. My counselor concluded there was nothing wrong with me. In our marriage, I was expected not to change or grow. My ex expected me to remain the same person I'd been at the start of the marriage almost two decades earlier. The constant comments from her during those years felt like death by a thousand cuts. From things she said before and after the divorce, I believed everything was my fault.

Towards the end of the marriage, my own depression grew. I hoped something would happen to me so I could never be a problem to anyone again. I thought if I became deathly ill or died in an accident, no one would be bothered by me again. While suicide was never an option to me, something medical would provide the same outcome. I also prayed someone would enter her life and sweep her off her feet. Either way, dead or divorced, I'd no longer be a problem in her life.

From the beginning of our relationship, my ex-spouse knew I cross-dressed, as the idea of transitioning was only a seed in my thoughts. It was an open subject before the proposal, though she never saw me dressed up. She said she was accepting of me, though after a few years it devolved into tolerance, then opposition to me being myself, as I was never allowed to present as my true self when anyone was in the house.

For most of my life, I was hurt by other's criticism. Hiding in the closet kept me closed off from enjoying life to its fullest. I was unable to trust people, so to avoid pain, I kept my thoughts and feelings to myself.

Only in my current marriage did cracks appear in the walls I'd built around me, allowing the first light to enter my closet. In my second marriage I finally have a family who accepts me for me. My wife and daughters' support broke the binds that held me in an unfulfilling life. The more I allow myself to step out as the woman I am at my soul, the lighter I become. Plus, as my skin gets softer, it also becomes more resistant. The comments and fears that once held me back no longer penetrate my defenses.

The cracks in the walls are growing. I'm now stepping out as my true self and opening up to others. Each step is significant to me, for as they compound, I'm able to walk further out the closet door. Yes, each step is a risk. However, they also seem guided, on a path set before me long ago.

I know God put people around me who follow the second great commandment, to love your neighbor as yourself, whether they know they are doing so or not. In a number of specific places, I am accepted—not just tolerated—for being the woman I've always been. In these settings, people's words are kind, their hearts are true, and they make me feel like a friend, not a freak. They talk with me on many levels, not just about the products being sold in their stores. I feel a true connection with each of them, and I look forward to the day when the masks go away, and I can exchange real smiles and hugs with them. They are the people who not only helped me grow, but they also helped me heal and get out of my suffocating closet. Many of my new friends tell me they've seen my confidence grow in the short time we've known each other. They are friends who've helped me regain my freedom through a journey of transition. Because of them, my growth has increased its pace over the past few months.

As for those who hurt me, I forgive them. Some of that pain was intentional, and some was unknown to those who hurt me. I will not forget what happened as I still feel many of those pains deeply. However, I found forgiveness is a key aspect of my transition process. I feel freer through forgiving others than I did when I refused to pardon their actions.

Finally, each person is unique. We were all placed in this world for a purpose. I prefer having the softer skin of a woman and helping people by being a friend rather than shaming others. Each of us needs positive support to be lifted up and cherished. That kind of care allows someone who feels no better than a weed in life to blossom into the most beautiful flower in God's creation. For me, that type of support led to my transition. Through amazing blessings, in the same way a caterpillar emerges from its cocoon, transition allowed me to emerge from my closet—beautiful and free, flying high like a butterfly.

20

November Reflections

By November, I was a mixed bag of emotions and contemplation. In a short six-week period, I went from feeling I was hiding my true self when I went out of the house in jeans, sneakers, and essentially unisex shirts, to wearing a dress and heels to the mall. My makeup regimen went from basic neutral looks to those that included a stunning self-made rose-gold eyeshadow, black eyeliner, mascara, and deep-red lipstick... all of which I wore when walking around the neighborhood.

My thoughts spun at the pace of my transition. By November, I needed to reflect on my changes thus far, my walk with God through transition, and the path where He was taking me. Before then, I focused on getting through life. I didn't sit down and ask myself, "How am I doing today?" or "What's changed since starting HRT?" It was time to consider those questions along with where I was headed.

Before August, I never had opportunities to comfortably hang out with other women. I always felt awkward. I conversed based on what I looked like, not who I was. From a young age, I saw a distinct differences in conversations between girls, boys, and mixed groups. Girls were more animated and seemed to talk about anything and everything while boys were stiff in their demeanor, showing both strength and emotional distance when interacting with one another. Then, in mixed company, group conversations became superficial and uninspiring. There were parameters around what could be discussed. I didn't fit in with the boys, so I stayed back and observed, fearing anything I said would get ridiculed. Until talking with the ladies in my favorite stores, I hadn't felt free to be open, talk about almost anything, and be treated as "one of the girls." Apart from the grocery store, there was no place for me to go and publicly interact with people as Susannah. My deepest wish was to go shopping for clothes and shoes, to use the advice other women gave about what looked good on me. It would be nice to go to a restaurant and hang out with those ladies. The pandemic muffled that possibility. It had to go on my "someday" wish list.

Thinking about the wish list, it's often easy to believe "wish" also means "will never happen." Just because I want to hang out with someone who I think is great and has been wonderful to me in the store doesn't mean they'll want—or have time—to hang out with me outside of the store. That's where my lack of understanding the nuances of social skills lie. Even when I worked for a large company, there were no lunch meetings nor times to hang out with coworkers, which left me feeling unwanted. However, I'm unwilling to believe those negative thoughts as I spent most of my life trying to pass as someone I wasn't, based solely on the body people saw. Now I'm living as the person I've always been and learning people actually do like me for me.

I learned this chatting with the associates in the stores. Quite often, different people would come right out and tell me they liked having me around. The way those ladies talked to me brought tears to my eyes. They told me my presence was something positive in their lives. I wasn't used to hearing those words. It was difficult to remember a time when anyone said something like that to me. It amplified how much they meant to me and helped me see other changes in myself now that I was living as the woman I'd always been inside.

One of the signs I was finally living as the woman I was meant to be occurred in November when I realized I was standing and walking taller. I used to slouch in my stance. Sometimes I wanted to look shorter around shorter people, but the root cause was low confidence and an inability to be myself. I lowered my head looking at the ground as I moved through life. In recent years, since I was still identifying as a male, slouching allowed me to hide the size of my breasts. Men didn't have breasts, at least not that were allowed to be visible without some potential for teasing. Breast size was another reason I often wore looser shirts.

Along with standing taller, my confidence increased. For decades I lacked confidence in myself, rarely seeing my successes. Imposter syndrome had a strong hold on me. However, especially in October, I began to blossom. By November, I had no second thoughts about getting out of the car wearing a skirt or dress when I left the house. Not only was I able to enter the grocery store and mall, I entered fast-food restaurants to place takeout orders, feeling comfortable about who I was and how I presented.

My ability to trust in myself as a woman only grew. There was a day at the mall when I felt like a couple ladies around my older daughter's age were looking at me in an odd way. It was as if they were trying to figure out who, or maybe what, I was. It was the type of scrutiny that worried me for much of my life, a fear that reared its ugly head whenever I thought about going out as my true self. However, because my confidence was growing with my transition, I was not bothered or worried by the way they looked at me.

By then, I presented myself as a woman in all facets of life, including my wardrobe, makeup, and actions. That helped boost my trust in myself, which I believed was a gift from God as He walked beside me through life. Yes, the ladies at MAC and Sephora were critical to the growth in my confidence. Their support and kindness was so important in encouraging me to feel safe in coming out. I also knew they wouldn't be in my life without the Lord putting them on my path.

~~~~~~

Actual Sephora survey comments from store visit
one day in November:

I love this Sephora store! I would not have the skincare and makeup skills I developed in recent months without the wonderful associates of this store. Also, from my first interaction in this specific store after last Christmas to now, the confidence to be myself that associates say they see in me would not exist.

Being an introvert, it can be difficult to accept the offered assistance or ask questions from associates I don't know. One of the reasons I like to visit Sephora is that I have a safe place to expand my comfort zone and do just that.

When I learn that my makeup catches someone's eyes and they then ask me how I did it, it's a great positive for me. That happened today when I was talking with Julie and noticed that she was fixated on my eye makeup. I showed her the Fenty palettes and shades I used today, including how both the yellow and red shimmer shades of the special palette helped to highlight colors. It was after I mentioned those two shades that she told me she could then see them on my eyelids. It was another conversation that made my day!

I know I often talk about how important Joy was at the start. She accepted me for being a woman from the beginning. She blazed the path for me to connect with others who became important to my growth. These women became safe friends I could talk to after Mom passed away. From the start, I found a safe place with safe people, where I was one of the girls.

My self-esteem was growing, and a sense of calm slowly covered me like a blanket on a warm winter night. I'd expanded my comfort zone so much since August, even with the craziness that was occurring throughout the country. Yet, there I was. I wasn't panicking about what people might think when they saw me, or how they might judge me. Instead, I centered on myself, letting my heart remain at peace so I could focus on daily life and the tasks at hand. I was relaxed.

As the sense of peace flowed over me, I was reminded of something I'd often told myself when I was very young. *I can do anything as a girl.* It was something I still truly believed.

During my reflections, memories from kindergarten rekindled. In my class, there were more boys than girls, so during gym activities like dancing,

I was placed with the girls. I had mixed emotions. I liked being one of the girls, but I knew I could not be seen enjoying the role for fear of being teased. The "sticks and stones" motto did nothing to mitigate my fears of being teased.

I also had strong memories of Revlon's commercials for Enjoli perfume during the early 1980s. I was mesmerized by the actress. She wore beautiful outfits and sang about how she could "bring home the bacon and fry it up in a pan." She could do anything, and I wanted to grow up to be like her. After all, I knew I could do anything as a woman. Even though I was never able to act upon it, I believed it through my high-school years, imagining I could do anything as a woman. I felt I was not able to do as much, or be as free, as a man. From my youth, I knew women could do anything, and I was one of them.

During that month of reflections, I also had periods of sadness. They popped up unexpectedly and were usually related to being alone, or feeling a fear of suppression.

The first occurred after talking with my youngest daughter. I absolutely adore her, and she was supposed to be with me for Christmas. Unfortunately, those plans, just like spring break and summer, were cancelled. It was already a year since we were last together. Continually extending our time apart disheartened me and tugged me down. She's one of my biggest supporters, and I missed her smile, hugs, and the love she always showed me.

The second was a realization that, for most of my life, no one seemed to care about my welfare or want to help me succeed. I was sad realizing I wasn't encouraged to chase my dreams in my youth. Being in a closet put blinders on me so I couldn't clearly see the rest of the world. While I felt alone, I knew it was possible there was help available and I just never saw it, never recognized an open hand for what it was. Age would become a part of my blinders. The older I got, the more difficult it became to see anyone being there for me.

I also remembered the comments of people during my youth, comments that led to me closing myself off from the world in the first place. I remembered the teasing, the unkind words that caused me to suppress myself until it became impossible to be the real me. By high school, I believed no one cared about, liked, or loved me.

When I originally wrote those thoughts, tears flowed. I wasn't angry with anyone for what happened, just sad. I'd coped the only way I knew how: I crawled deeper into an internal hole, further into the closet, to protect me from the pain. I was an introvert, left to try and figure out life on my own. There was no one else I could turn to for help.

Then I thought of what happened during the past year. I remembered how people I didn't know smiled and talked with me like a friend. Again, tears flowed as I saw the lies of my past slowly erased by the truths of the present. The people at Sephora and MAC showed me I had value, that people beyond my immediate family cared about me. It helped expunge decades of despair. When I had sad news, there were friends who would listen and check in to make sure I was doing alright. When I had good news, those same friends were there to celebrate with me. Standing taller with more confidence had much to do with those new friends.

And while I had many new friends, November was about to bring someone into my life who would rock my world in a very positive way.

21

And Then There Was Heather...

In early November, I had a chance encounter with the district director for my Sephora store. I was headed towards the mall exit, walking with Betsy who was going to a coffee stand. Betsy began waving to a blonde lady a little shorter than me as she moved towards us. That's when I met Heather.

Recently, I had talked with Betsy about an idea for a writing project. When she introduced me to Heather, Betsy told her we were talking about collaborating.

Even though Heather made an immediate and positive impact on me when we met, I had butterflies in my stomach during the introduction. Her personality was very caring. She accepted me as Betsy's friend, and the two of them talked openly in front of me, as though I was part of the conversation even though it had nothing to do with me. Heather was very stylish. I found myself admiring the waves in her hair, hoping that some-day I might have a similar style.

Being with Betsy, I was slightly more open about myself and my back-ground than if I had met Heather on my own in a different setting. I can't recall much of the conversation, although I told Betsy afterwards that I really liked Heather. I was a bit quiet during that first meeting, so I re-minded Betsy of how shy I become when meeting people for the first time.

It was a couple weeks later, on Black Friday, when I saw Heather again. It became one of the most amazing, uplifting, and eye-opening conversations I'd had in a long time.

Ever since the first Sephora survey I did in August, I tried to complete a survey for every purchase. Often, my surveys included stories of things that made my day or were new aspects of my transitional growth. It was important to me to be transparent, as surveys were also another way for me to let my friends know how much I valued them.

Heather said hi when she saw me near the center station. I took a few seconds to recognize her as it was only our second meeting, and this time it was just the two of us. Heather told me she read all the purchase survey comments, and that she also knows specifically when I submit comments. I knew the associates were adept at identifying my notes. I had no idea anyone above the store level read them, much less could tell which were mine. While that tidbit amazed me, it was what Heather told me next that floored me, making my day in a way I never expected.

"I had no idea you weren't born a female until you said something." She reminded me of our first meeting, and I quickly tried to recap that time, but to no avail. In hindsight, if she really knew those were my comments, it's possible that was how she knew.

"I've never really known how I present when I'm out of the house," I said. "You're the very first person to tell me that I present as a woman in public."

"I believe that everyone who sees you walking around in the mall sees you as just another woman."

I was so surprised to hear those words, especially from someone I'd only met for about five minutes a few weeks earlier!

I told her briefly how Thanksgiving was a bit up and down for me. I'd never had friends to hang out with, although the ladies in Sephora were starting to feel like that to me. My biggest concern was that I might be too open and say too much when talking with them.

That was when Heather told me how many of the associates saw me as one of them in the store, like part of the team. She said they enjoyed when I showed up.

It felt so good to hear that! It was one of the few times anyone said something that allowed me think I made a difference in the lives of others. I looked up to the ladies in Sephora as though they were my older sisters, helping and guiding me in makeup and skincare.

Over the next few months, I crossed paths with Heather three times.

The first was a couple weeks after her amazing words. Walking around Sephora, I saw her talking with some of the associates. I wanted to chat with her, yet she was busy, and it was difficult for me to just walk up and interrupt a conversation. She had been kind and open with me, yet the introvert inside held me back. Instead, I looked at some of the different makeup brands. While I was in the Make Up For Ever section, she came over and spoke with me.

"You should try those Make Up For Ever sparkle lipsticks," she said, noting the ones on sale.

"I've got so many MAC lipsticks," I said, "plus I recently bought the Sephora lip stain collection. I'm not sure that I really need any more lipstick right now."

As we talked, I let her know my website was live and showed her the first photo on the site. She said she loved my lip color.

"It's a Sephora lip gloss, the first lip gloss I've ever had," I replied.

When she noticed the grey calf-height wedge slouch boots I was wearing, she commented on how good they looked and asked where I got them. I told her, mentioning I was not sure about the pointed toes as my preference was for round-toe shoes and boots.

"The pointed toes help make legs look longer," she said, although we both already knew I had long legs.

"I do like them," I said, "especially as I need larger sizes and wide calf boots. Fortunately, Cheyenne told me about the site where I found them, and they're reasonably priced."

After I got home that day, I wrote in my diary: "I LOVE talking with Heather. She is always so cheerful and confident." Speaking with Heather and hearing her positive words about me erased years of pain and negative words. Hearing such positive comments about me was so new. It was difficult at times to believe such kind words were directed towards me.

It would be another couple of months, not until February 2021, before I saw Heather again. Whenever I thought about her, her positive and supportive words still amazed me. Our paths crossed at a new store opening. I was in the vicinity for a manicure appointment—my second manicure ever! Heather immediately recognized me as I walked over to her. I knew she was busy with the store opening activities, yet she still took some time to chat.

"You always look put together," she said as she looked at what I wore that day. I had on black leggings, a tan tunic with a red reindeer pattern, and black knee-high boots.

Thanking her, I pulled up two day-after-Christmas photos that were taken exactly one year apart. I wore the same outfit and glasses in each, as a way to see how much I'd changed during the year. Not only was she amazed at the difference, Heather commented on how good my skin looked.

"It's all Sephora," I replied.

Heather responded by saying that my experience with Sephora and the associates who watched me grow over the past year was what Sephora was meant to be. What happened to me over the past year, and especially the last few months, was the type of experience everyone should have with their stores.

"You know that you really are a member of the other store's family, and that they'll expect you to stay with them." Heather was direct on that point.

"I could never leave them," I said. "They're so important to me, and I could never have done this without them."

Then I added, "It was your fault I ended up buying all five of the Make Up For Ever sparkle lipsticks when they were on sale."

"My fault?"

"You planted the seed. Once they went on sale after Christmas, I started with two, then somehow ended up working my way through to buy each color until I had them all. On top of that, they really do look good on me."

When we crossed paths a couple times in the store that day, Heather introduced me to people she knew. The first was an honorary guest, Lynn, who was there for the opening. Like Heather, Lynn was a statuesque blonde who looked to be slightly taller than me. Heather introduced me to her, and I tried to recognize the lady Heather was describing to Lynn... until I realized it was me! Heather sees the best in people, and that's what she conveyed in her introductions. It's such an amazing feeling to hear others openly speak positive things about me. When I stood with both of those beautiful, very feminine ladies, instead of feeling in awe of them, I felt like I fit in and was part of the conversation.

The second lady Heather introduced me to was Miriam, a product rep who was there for the opening. I needed to find one item so my purchase would qualify for a free Sephora bag and was directed to that section of the store for a product promotion. As I neared the section, Heather saw me and asked what I was getting. I showed her, mentioning what I needed, and she quickly introduced me to Miriam, telling me she was often at my Sephora store.

Again, as she made the introductions, Heather was generous in how she talked about me.

Again, I was amazed at her supportive words.

For so much of my life, I felt alone and on my own. I stayed out of the way at family events and found it difficult to make friends. Rarely, was there a time when I could hang out with anyone and enjoy a safe environment. I believed I had to do everything by myself. I had difficulty asking for help. I felt no one paid attention to me, as though I was expected to have answers to my own questions. That only made it harder to come up with questions. My journey had always been one taken alone.

However, heading into the holiday season, it seemed I was finding the friends and family I had desired for so many years.

22

Finding Friends and Family

My life was filled with acquaintances. You know the type. They're the people who pass through your life due to work, school, church, or where you live. They know your name, and you know theirs, yet in many ways that's the extent of the connection. You only knew each other because life put you in the same place at the same time. You might talk for a few minutes, though without depth. There was no reason to hang out, invite them to dinner or a barbeque, or go for a walk in the park.

Once the situation that brought you together ended, so did the connection. You went to different workplaces, moved to different neighborhoods, or had kids and changed your schedule which reduced your availability to get to know others. Maybe you were in the military, and once out, there was no real reason to continue those connections since you never talked with them in any depth when you served together.

That's my life. I don't recall having any close friends. I've met lots of people through school, work, church, and the military, yet there were no true connections, no friendships of lasting substance. Most conversations were superficial or work focused. The people in my life were acquaintances, and once our paths diverged, there was no more contact, only memories. Although some of those memories were positive, they were only that, memories.

My definition of friend is someone you enjoy being with, who is genuine, transparent, and shares something about themself. Friends are non-judgmental. There were times when I said more about myself than maybe I should have, yet that's part of trying to find potential friends—those who are also willing to be honest and open with me.

That's some of what was happening with my friends at the mall. I was finding unexpected connections with other women. Often, especially in Sephora, the associates said I wasn't just a customer; they viewed me as part of their family. Those were words I'd longed to hear most of my life! I found other women who were amazingly wonderful, creating a place where I could put the cares of the world behind me once I crossed the threshold into the store.

Where those friendships will go is yet to be determined. COVID, and the fact that everyone keeps their distance, makes it more difficult to gather as a group and get to know each other beyond the atmosphere of the store. However, a key aspect of a friend is how they are there for you and are up front about saying so. Some of the ladies at Sephora told me they are there for me if I need them.

I've never had friends I felt I could trust. If someone asked how I was doing, I'd give a simple, "Fine," and that was the end of the conversation. I never felt safe letting anyone know I was having a hard time. To do so felt like I was a burden. The feeling was validated a few years ago when I took someone at their word about being able to let them know if anything was wrong. I called the person one night to let them know I was driving to the ER because my home blood pressure monitor said my BP was over 200 (the ER measured it at 250ish / 190ish). I left them a message at 10 pm, and never heard back, not even to check to see if I was alright. To me, it was confirmation that I wasn't important.

That began to change at the end of October. There was a day when Jeanette was out front monitoring the line at Sephora. When she saw me, she said, "You're something of a celebrity in the store."

I about blushed right there. I was finally hearing words of validation, finding out people not only knew me, but they also cared about me. Her words let me know the associates in the store knew me. Over the next few months, multiple beauty advisors told me they loved to see me in the store and how I made their days. Friendships were blossoming with people I had only known for a couple months, and it felt good!

At Sephora, I was finding friends. I'm often transparent about myself with those I've known the longest. They know I'm on HRT. I've learned how to explain to others what I'm going through, and to answer questions as honestly as possible. I've also found that having at least a few people at Sephora know about my HRT was important when it came to my skin-care routine. I'd always had more of an oily complexion, and never thought twice about it. However, when I found that my foundation was drying up and looking cracked after just a few hours, I turned to the ladies who knew me best to help identify a solution. First off, I'd purchased a mattifying moisturizer prior to the start of my problems. When walking through the possible causes of why there was such a finish problem, one of my friends helped come up with a combination of two likely candidates: HRT and the new product. She knew I was on hormones and told me they can constantly change the skin. In my case, my skin was getting dryer, so the new product was wrong for me. Once it was out of my routine, I added a couple products designed to increase moisture and the problem disappeared.

I learned which ladies I could open up with, to let them know when I was going through difficult times. Prior to the past year, when one of those emotional roller coasters took off with me on it, my response was to pull away from everyone, including the people I loved. That began to change when I learned there were a handful of people I could trust and be genuine with. During one of the earlier emotional periods, my fears rose, and I was scared about pulling away from people I was just getting to know and were already so important to me. When I opened up to a couple associates, their love and verbal support came through. Just a few simple words helped me feel better. Others have opened up to me about situations in their own lives, letting me into their worlds. I felt a true sense of trust from them. With many of the beauty advisors, the connection is not as deep; conversations remain focused on cosmetics and skincare. Others, however, have evolved into connections that feel like the start of real friendships.

By the end of November, I completed five months of HRT. There was a smoothness to my facial skin that became more noticeable, especially after shaving. I could feel a softness that wasn't there before. My cheeks were becoming plumper and more visible. For the first time, I felt I was in my correct skin. It wasn't the tough skin I'd lived with for most of my life. My skin felt light and airy, giving me a sense of peace.

23

Shaking the Holiday Blues

In many ways, Thanksgiving was the start of one of those emotional roller-coaster rides, a ride which lasted through the holiday season. By that point, it had been eight months since I'd had a hug, eight months of being alone. I was lonely. There was no one I felt comfortable and safe to talk with, no friends to sit down and check in with, no one around with whom to cry if need be.

Even though I knew I could open up with my wife and daughters, there was also nothing they could do as each was over a thousand miles away. I didn't want to needlessly worry them about how I was doing. I knew I'd get through the rough times. I was good at forging through tough times on my own. I'd been doing it all my life.

It still didn't change the fact that what I wanted—needed—was a friend with whom I could talk, confide, and reciprocate.

On Thanksgiving, I made a full-blown nineteen-pound turkey (it was the cheapest option by cost per pound) dinner with all the trimmings... for one. At least it meant lots of leftovers, thereby covering my meals for the next week. The bird was stuffed and in the oven first thing in the morning. After breakfast, I sat down to frost the Christmas cookies I baked the previous night. Soon after I started frosting, the morning devolved into a crying session which continued sporadically all day.

It's so easy to let the mind wander when alone doing simple tasks like frosting cookies. My thoughts returned to how I didn't remember having any friends. Most of the time I was fine being alone. No one beyond my wife and daughters was close enough for me to invite them over. Due to my transition and talking with different beauty advisors, that was changing. There were several ladies at Sephora who were beginning to feel like real friends, not just acquaintances. Marie, Julie, Carol, Laura, Cheyenne, Betsy, Brenda, Katie, and so many others were people I adored, ladies around whom I felt liked, cared about, and possibly loved. Those tears were filled with joy over the realization that, finally, I wasn't as alone as I felt.

And yet, other tears flowed for the simple reason that I was never comfortable interacting with people, always unsure of what to say or do around them. I usually stayed in the background and observed my surroundings, afraid to interact with others in case I said the wrong thing or talked too much. I tearfully prayed for help developing stronger and deeper friendships with others. What was appropriate to say during the early phases of a budding friendship? Part of me wished I had offered to have people come over during Thanksgiving week, yet it also felt wrong to even consider it due to COVID and health concerns. It would have been fun to have others over to bake cookies, make fudge, or just watch a movie.

Even though my dad was nearby, we both agreed it was best not to get together for Thanksgiving dinner. As much as I loved him and the rest of my family, I still felt lonely around them. Growing up, I was never close with my parents or brothers. I had already started to shut myself off from them when my dad began asking me during supper, "Did you learn anything in school today, or do you have to go back tomorrow?" I was only eight, and didn't understand he was trying to be humorous, trying to interact with me. Instead, my interpretation was that it really didn't matter what I learned since I had to go to school the next day, anyway.

I cried, knowing I had to pretend to be who my family expected me to be when we were together. That played a significant part in the ping-pong game going on in my head about how I could and should present in public. I knew I was female, that I've always been one of the girls. There were often times I was uncomfortable, and even afraid of men and being around them. It was partly based on the relationship with my dad who believed that to spare the rod would spoil the child. As I frosted one cookie after another, I looked forward to the day I could be around my family as the woman I've always known I am: Susannah. It's taken so long to emerge from my cocoon of a closet.

I cried for Mom. I was still grieving. Although she hadn't been part of Thanksgiving dinner for five years, thinking of her and how we made Thanksgiving dinner together for so many years before she entered memory care was overwhelming. It was an odd sense. I could start crying saying, "I miss my mom," and at the same time continue frosting the cookie in my hand.

Thus, on Black Friday, I went to the one place where everybody seemed to know my name: Sephora. That was the second time I met Heather, the day she told me everyone in the store felt like I was one of them. Before I left, I had spoken with a dozen different beauty advisors—friends, talking about everything from skincare to cosmetics to what I had already purchased at sales in other stores. While Thanksgiving was an off day for me, when I left Sephora on Friday, I felt much better about myself.

One odd, yet also affirming, event occurred in early December at a vendor kiosk in the mall. A lady offered me a sample of a skincare product, which somehow opened the door for her to have me sit me down. Then she began to place a sample of a wrinkle cream under one of my eyes. She was pleasant as she talked to me, though I wasn't sure how to take her comment that something about my eyes caught her interest. She kept asking me to lower my mask. I refused.

The affirming part came from one specific question. She asked if I was married, to which I said yes. Then she asked about my husband. I didn't answer her, though I smiled to myself under the mask. Even with my bigger hands and worries about how my voice came across, she still assumed I was just another married woman in the mall. At no time did she say anything that seemed like she was questioning my birth gender, which made my day. It felt wonderful to have her comment and treat me as any other beautiful lady who passed her kiosk, even though the skeptical part of me suspects many of her comments were to close a sale.

As for her product, it wasn't for me. It did have a tightening effect under my eyes that made them appear smoother. However, the feeling was very dry, almost like paper, in the areas where it was applied. It was easy to leave without buying the product for two reasons. First, she kept lowering the price, which meant it was overpriced to begin with. Second, the result on my skin was not pleasant at all. There was no way I was going to spend money on her product.

It was becoming easier for me to accept that others saw me as just another lady. I noticed myself doing little things that I avoided just a few months earlier. One example was when a package was delivered to my home. Usually, if the delivery person knocked on my door, I waited until they drove off before quickly stepping out to get it. On that day, I wore blue leggings, a multi-colored pink sweater, and a pink hairband. When I stepped outside to pick up the package, I saw it wasn't addressed to me. Making sure my door was unlocked, I started towards the sidewalk to take the package to the delivery truck when the driver came back around the corner with my package. While he saw me, we exchanged the packages without making any comments or facial expressions.

The key point was that I didn't think twice about how I looked, and my actions were automatic: to find the delivery person to return the package. After I entered the house, I realized what happened. I'd taken another step towards being the genuine me, not thinking about what others saw and just being the best me possible. The reality was that most people didn't even think twice when they saw me. I rarely noticed anyone stare or do a double take. I had taken the next steps in affirming my identity. As one song I love says, "in my armor I'm bulletproof in the face of others, especially those who may look down on me."

I was starting to live my life, unworried about what others thought. It was a testament to how I was treated at Sephora. Thus, with the approach of Christmas, I wanted to give my friends a card to let them know how much they meant to me during that Christmas season. Slipping it to Betsy, she asked, "Will it make me cry?"

Since I was unsure, I remained silent. She came back a few minutes later and said it brought tears to her eyes.

~~~~~~

Christmas Card—2021—to all the Sephora Associates

My heartfelt wish is for each of you to have a happy and joyous Christmas this year.

You've all been so wonderful, helping me in ways I never expected. Each of you played a significant role in my growth this year, for which I'm very thankful.

You helped a socially awkward girl in an awkward year of so many transitions to feel welcome, gain confidence, and be more open. You were there to help me grow my skincare and makeup skills, giving me the verbal pictures I needed to understand so many facets in this new area of my life. You were there with both kind words and acts at the times I needed a friend, whether you actually knew I was down or not. You always provided the smiles (behind the mask, of course) and eye twinkles that picked me up.

I have no regrets that life transitioned when it did. I believe that God set my path and timeline to ensure we would meet, for it was only during this time that I could have met all of you and felt the warmth you've given me this past year. For that, I feel truly blessed and loved.

To each of you I give a virtual hug.

Merry Christmas,
Susannah Dawn

~~~~~~

During that same visit, Laura was dressed as the Grinch. It was fun to see the excitement of the kids when they saw her. Even some of the parents and teenagers seemed to have fun with the Grinch. Before leaving the store, Cheyenne took many photos of me with "Grinch" Laura. While I had fun doing the photos, I quickly realized I was still fairly rigid in front of a camera. While Laura made lots of different poses, I hardly changed my stance. Inside, I felt the desire to move about and have fun with the pictures, yet my stoic body was stuck in a stiff display carried over from childhood. The free-spirited girl was still trying to fight her way into the light to take the loose, carefree photos she used to take before beginning her exile in the closet. It was something with which I needed help and encouragement: being open and flowing in front of a camera.

In the end, I knew that just taking the photos with Laura was a huge step. I'm not sure I'd have even considered it as an option in August. It was important to realize how far I'd already come, to be free of the shackles that held me back for so long. If I was able to wear a dress to Sephora, I know one day I'll be able to take happy and genuine photos that show the real me.

I believe.

24

Christmas and Looking Back Over a Year of Change

Christmas wasn't as tough as Thanksgiving. I cooked another large turkey dinner, giving myself another week's worth of leftovers, which was the best part, anyway. I looked forward to having more "Thanksgiving Leftover Burritos." I came up with the creation after Thanksgiving: burrito tortillas with heated leftovers rolled up inside. One thing about the pandemic was the creation of new meal ideas.

The best part of Christmas day was the video call with my youngest daughter when we opened our Christmas gifts! She's such a blessing in my life, and I've loved her through thick and thin. The video call was her idea, beating me to the punch. We talked about what she'd already received for Christmas and how we were both doing. We took turns opening gifts. She only opened the gifts that were from me, while I opened all my gifts during that call. I'd gotten myself a few things since it was just me at home, plus I had a present from a brother. As with all our calls, we had a great time. They never happen as often as I'd like, yet I never push for more as she's got a lot on her plate with school.

The day after Christmas was also special. I left home wearing the same sweater and glasses as I had the day I met Joy, exactly one year earlier. I used the same foundation and eyeshadow she put on me that day, but styled them a bit differently due to my improved skills. I added a darker blush, mascara, eye liner, and highlighter. Before I left, I took photos to chronicle the changes.

The difference was like night and day!

I showed the side-by-side photos on my phone to everyone in Sephora and MAC, telling them about my first day with Joy.

In MAC, Linda remembered that day. She watched me change over the year but hadn't realized the transformation was so dramatic. Lori, too, was amazed at the difference.

It took a few visits to Sephora before everyone saw the photos. I told them, "These changes are a direct result of all of you. I couldn't have done it without you."

Laura was at the entrance when I arrived, so I showed her first. She was amazed at the change. Carol was next, and after telling her the story about Joy, she couldn't believe the transformation, either. Cheyenne, Betsy, Nikki, Linda, Zoe, Brenda, Cara... they were all surprised to see the differences between the photos.

Then I showed Wendy. She said my skincare made the difference between the photos. She was surprised at the change, especially in my cheeks. Since I was almost six months on HRT, I suggested there might have been other "assistance" to help them fill out.

Marie gushed how happy she was to see the changes and growth! Ever since we met in October, she was one of the biggest supporters of my transition. Every time she saw me, she checked in to make sure I was doing alright.

Then there was Vanessa. She was shorter than Joy, with wavy lighter-brown hair. When I showed her the photos, Vanessa said she remembered that day. We originally talked about it back in November, when I had a chance to finally chat with her at the entrance as I left. When I mentioned Joy and showed her the photo from that first day, Vanessa recalled Joy telling her, "It's her first time having makeup put on her." That also reminded me how Joy was the first person to use she / her pronouns when talking about me.

A couple days later, I saw Julie. I was standing beside her at the central counter area. Her first words were, "Where's the photos?!" Everyone was aware of the photos showing the extent of my transformation over the past year. Julie was blown away! She also pointed out that my face was thinner in the current photo.

Jeanette said it looked like I'd had a face lift, while Deborah was amazed at the difference. Debbie echoed something that many in the store said to me. When I was adamant the credit for my changes, especially skincare, went to everyone at Sephora, she responded, "It was all you." I didn't argue with her, since it was obvious I wouldn't win.

However, I was right. I listened to each beauty advisor, following their recommendations for the products I purchased. Without their knowledge and guidance, I had no idea what I was doing or how to use the products correctly. Many people watch YouTube videos for instructions on makeup and skincare routines and application. That didn't work for me. I needed the personal interactions in the store to ask questions, make sure I understood what they said, and follow their lead. There were times a product didn't work the way I wanted, or I altered their guidance slightly, though that was rare. I usually told the associates, "I do what you tell me to do."

I wrote a special survey comment about my day-after-Christmas visit.

~~~~~~

Actual Sephora survey comments from my store visit on 26 December 2020:

Today included one important story that is very personal for me, and yet would never have occurred without the friends (though so many feel more like family) that I've made at this Sephora store... and while I will provide the short version, I am available to provide the long version for those who ask.

One this exact day last year, 26 Dec 2019, I was color matched for foundation and had eyeshadow put on me for the first time, which Joy so lovingly did for me. Before leaving the store, she offered to remove the makeup or leave it on me, and I chose to leave the store with my makeup on to walk through the mall. Today, I wore the same sweater and glasses as that day a year ago to see if there was any difference between then and now. Having a photo from after I got home that day a year ago, I took an "updated" photo today before leaving home this morning, I had untouched photographical evidence of how much I've changed during the past year, which I know in my heart is a direct result of the love I've felt in this store.

Vanessa was there that day a year ago, when Joy became the first person to both help me with makeup and was the first person to refer to me as "she"—for I heard Joy say it in reference to me when talking with another associate, who happened to be Vanessa! I know that at least a handful of associates specifically remember me from that time period (Dec 2019 – Feb 2020), including Marie, Brenda, and Cheyenne. A year ago, I had blinders on when entering the store, always looking for Joy first, and talking with Brenda, Morgan, and only a couple other associates. Now I feel comfortable talking with almost everyone in the store—while wearing a dress (though there are still a few associates—primarily the newer ones—I have not really interacted with... yet).

The true blessing to me from today was the positive, excited reactions I received from those who saw the two photos side-by-side... even I was unaware of the true change until today. I'm so grateful that everyone I've met and gotten to know over this past year has been so kind and helpful with this transition (though most of those interactions really occurred from August to now). I truly feel I could not have achieved this without each and every one of them... and I can say that I personally know almost 30 associates and reps in this Sephora store! I love them all!

~~~~~~~~~~~~~~~~~~~~~~~~~~~~~~~~~~~~

I spent New Year's Eve day with Lauren and Allison when they passed through town. Our text and email conversations had picked up in recent months, especially after Mom's death. I updated them on almost everything that happened with me, at least what I thought they'd want to know. I was surprised and glad that Lauren invited me in December to watch an online concert by students in her non-profit music program. There were some talented kids, and I'm glad they were able to continue their music lessons during COVID.

The three of us went for a walk near my house. It was the first time I comfortably dressed as my true self around them, wearing knee-high boots and skinny jeans. The weather cooperated to let us walk without getting wet, though it was very much on the colder side. I was excited to see them both and get some time to hang out. It was a chance to catch up while letting them see the real me for the first time. After they returned to their home, I received the most wonderful note from Lauren:

I want you to know that though you came to be family through marriages, you are really our chosen family as well. That's something that Allison said after we visited at Christmas time and has really resonated with me. You are our chosen family. Thank you for being you and allowing us into your life. Truly grateful.

I teared up reading those words. I've struggled for much of my life to figure out where I belonged, who I could trust and be open with, and who wouldn't hurt me for doing so. I never felt like I belonged with my family. It's been hard to trust any of them because of how I got hurt in the past. However, the five special women who came late into my life showed me love for who I am, and for that I'm truly grateful.

After Lauren and Allison left, I had a quiet New Year's Eve. I spent the night watching movies, eating popcorn, and waiting for 2020 to end. Though there were many reasons to view 2020 as one of the worst years in a long time, for me, there were many positives.

2020 was the first time I went out in public alone as Susannah. Though I was scared the first few months, the support I received from Sephora kept me moving forward. Most, if not all, of the associates knew I was a trans woman, and they always accepted me. There were times we talked and they seemed to even forget that little detail. Reminding them I was new to cosmetics and skincare seemed to jog their memories. Many have become good friends, and I hope a time will come when we have opportunities to hang out together, maskless, outside of the store setting. I also hope that as associates leave for new opportunities, they won't forget me and will keep in touch. Now that I've had a chance to get to know them and to know their hearts, I don't want to lose them from my life. They're all included in my prayers.

25

ESSAY: What It Feels Like to Be a Trans Woman

What It Feels Like to be a Trans Woman

A Personal Essay by Susannah Dawn

One of the hardest things to explain to people is what it feels like to be a trans woman. I can talk about how I knew by age three I was a girl, still vividly remembering saying my nightly prayers to God so long ago, asking Him to let me wake up a girl. I can explain how nothing I did during the next half century—while trying to identify as a male—changed my fundamental knowledge, or the definite need to be able to transition and live life as my true self.

I get it.

In this world, the vast majority of people are comfortable knowing how both their core self and bodies align. They were born into the correct body, so it is virtually impossible for them to even imagine life any other way. When you are comfortable in your skin, the natural expectation is to believe everyone should feel the same way. For most men, the thought of wanting to be a woman seems inconceivable, an abomination... just ask my dad. He cringed at the thought of anything outside his idea of what the norm should be, including me. The day I told him I was trans, something I needed to do for myself, was the last time we spoke.

Over the last year, I've come out to many people from my past, and most accept me for being the woman I have always been. They support me with their friendship and kind words. Yet there are still many in this world who seem to question the validity of trans people, often arguing against the rights of trans people. Those opposed to the transgender community are found amongst all walks of life, including leadership and government positions. Their actions create a sense of preferring to view trans people as abnormal, abominations that threaten what they perceive as the moral norms of humanity.

The real problem, as I see it, is how opponents may not have met and actually gotten to know a trans person… at least not that they were aware of. Their viewpoints in opposition of accepting trans people are likely based on their perception of vocal trans figures and activists who could be considered extreme amongst the trans community. When the narrative focuses on the most visible and perceived-outlandish trans people as representing an entire group, it makes it easier for opponents to use that image to describe the whole community as immoral people pressuring leaders to do what they request. In turn, it leads those same opponents to write legislation that tries to restrict the constitutional rights of a specific group of Americans.

It's difficult for non-trans people to even fathom what it's like to be a trans woman. Consider allies or opponents, politicians from any point along the political spectrum, anyone in the LGBTQ sphere, religious leaders, or anyone else who is not a trans person. How can they comprehend what it's like to be a trans woman, trapped in a body requiring transition so her soul, her true persona, and her body finally align?

Let me paint a picture to help describe what it means for me to be a trans woman, to finally transition and live my life with the freedom of being my true female self.

Imagine a person who is bound and has their mouth covered with tape so they can't scream—it's an image we've seen a thousand times in movies and televisions shows. In this case, the person with tape over her mouth is named "Jill." "Jack" will be the person taping Jill's mouth shut.

When Jack places the tape over Jill's mouth to keep her quiet, he expects she will easily breathe through her nose. Most likely, he wouldn't see any problems in covering her mouth with tape. Based on his personal experience, Jack never had problems breathing through just his nose. Thus, he is unable to consider how covering the mouth could be a problem—an issue—when someone is forced to breathe solely through their nose.

The thing is, Jill has sinus issues that habitually impacted her ability to breathe solely through her nose. Often during her life, Jill's sinuses would fill up, or her nasal passages would have some type of slow blockage requiring her to breathe through her mouth. And so, after Jill's mouth is taped shut, her nasal passages begin to narrow as something gradually obstructs them. Her air supply becomes restricted and she's unable to breathe in life-giving air in the quantity needed. Anxiety, fear, and panic set in as she's trapped with no way to free herself. It leads to a rise in Jill's heart rate, followed by the need for an increase in breathable airflow. The longer the tape is on, the longer the angst of being trapped fills Jill, and the more her panic rises. She must be released so she can easily breathe in the air so necessary for life, yet the tape also inhibits her ability to clearly articulate her need.

Though Jack may see Jill squirm due to her panic, he chalks it up to Jill struggling to get herself free, not an inability to breath. When she begins to subside in her struggles, Jack figures she tired herself out or resigned herself to her condition of being trapped.

Yet for Jill, the situation is much grimmer. From her reduced breathing capacity, she passes out, which could mean her slow death. The entire time, Jack is oblivious to her true condition.

Being trapped in my body while knowing who I really am is like Jill's situation. Having to hide away in the closet, to not be who I was created to be, is like having my mouth taped while my nasal passages slowly become blocked, unable to easily breathe. I struggle to fit inside a box labeled "male" and slowly suffocate. The tape is symbolic of the fear of what others might think if I came out as a trans woman, so I continue struggling to breathe inside a confined space. The longer I'm unable to live as my true self, the more likely I am to remain withdrawn from a world that does not seem to accept me. It leads to anxiety, fear, and potentially, death.

Throughout my life, my faith kept me from succumbing to the fear and panic I felt inside me and in that box. Faith kept me alive inside a dark closet where suicide would be so easy, as death would remove the pain holding me back from living a full life.

Jack is like those who don't understand how someone can be trans, let alone the need to transition. They can easily breathe with their mouth covered, live perfectly fine within a body aligned with who they are at their core self. When trans people are forced to stay hidden due to feeling the world is an unsafe place to exit their closet, their visible numbers remain very low. The Jacks of the world likely feel a sense of justification that the issue of individuals claiming to be transgender was not really what the trans activists made it out to be, that it's an anomaly they can legislate into oblivion.

Yet each of us is unique, created differently, and we are all made in the image of God.

People who never experienced the feeling of not aligning with their body often find it difficult to understand how being trans is real, how it's a significant part of who I am, and how I was fearfully and wonderfully created this way in my mother's womb. Being able to publicly live as my true self is like having the tape removed and breathing in the life-giving air necessary to survive and thrive instead of trying to breathe with blocked nostrils in a stifling closet.

When I felt forced to hide, forced to identify—to live—as something I was not at my core, it was like losing the ability to breathe. Yet through it all, both in that closet and then exiting through the doors opened by the Lord, I never lost sight of a basic truth:

God never makes mistakes.

God made me the way I am for a reason. I understood early on, at the age of three, I was a girl. However, the Lord had a reason for me to be hidden away over the next half century. He knew the difficulties I would face, both in what pushed me into that closet and the subsequent years I spent there, yet the Lord also knew my closet would be transformed into a cocoon from which I would finally emerge as the woman I am today. He made me this way for a reason and opened the doors for me to emerge as my true self. The Lord showed me how love is so much greater than anything else in this world.

When the tape was put over my mouth, like Jill, I felt fear and panic. The world kept that tape in place. I felt unsafe to step out into it and let people know the real me. Hiding my true self made it hard for me to connect with people and difficult to make any real friends. I slipped into a foggy state of existing instead of growing. I was unable to believe in my abilities as they were hidden in the closet with my core being. It wasn't until the Lord began to open doors, to place people in my life who accepted and supported me as the woman I always knew He created me to be, when the fog began to lift, the tape fell away, and I could once again breathe deeply.

It's difficult to breathe as a trans woman who feels forced to hide from the rest of the world in order to feel safe. It makes stepping into the world as my true self difficult. It took time to get here, including a half century living with that tape over my mouth and a diminished ability to breathe all those years. Yet the tape finally came off. I opened up to people I felt might be safe, and found they were more than safe... they asked to stay with me on my journey, becoming my support group and awesome friends—real friends.

With the tape gone, no longer suffocating me, I also realized something I always knew: as a woman, I can fly.

26

Into the New Year

H eading into 2021 brought with it hopes and dreams of a year that would be better than the one that just ended.

One Christmas gift I gave myself was a photo book of my transition during 2020. It was a way for me to see the extent of transformation that occurred since meeting Joy. It also provided me a sense of when changes happened. Even though those first photos of me looked rough and unpolished, it was still me as I began a journey that will last a lifetime. There was a photo from when I began HRT. Photos of how I looked in August when I was around family after Mom passed away. Photos from my first time out in a skirt, in a dress, and a series of photos I called "Eye-volution" to show how my eye-makeup skills had grown. There was even a set of photos to provide a simple recap across two pages of what I looked like through the year, in chronological order. The photos of me in the same sweater outfit that I wore exactly one year apart bookended them.

Seeing the physical changes was one thing. Seeing my emotional growth and how it steadily improved my confidence was something else. My friends noticed it when they saw the pictures of me through the year. Katie was one of the first to say I looked more confident over the last four months of the year: both in the photos and in person. I didn't understand the truth to her words until I saw the photos and realized how much I had truly stepped out on my own. My fears were lessening as I strengthened my faith through the process. I couldn't have taken so many steps out of that dark closet without the help of the wonderful associates at Sephora and MAC who befriended and supported me. I would never have met those wonderful people if God hadn't put them on my path. That was where my faith lay. That's why I could grow so much, so quickly.

I kept the book in my purse, knowing many of my friends wanted to see it. I also knew it would take a while to let them all see it. What I didn't expect was how, over time, it simply became known as "The Book." Many of the ladies asked if it was available for sale... and if I would sign and leave the copy I carried in my purse for them to keep in the store!

Watching their reactions helped me feel better as myself. It validated the changes throughout my journey. Betsy took her time to make sure she didn't miss one page or photo, often commenting on how much I'd grown over the year. When I saw Julie for the first time since bringing the book to the store, she didn't say hello or how are you. Instead, while it was in Sally's hands, Julie blurted out, "Is that The Book?" She not only joined Sally in looking at it but had positive comments for almost every photo. Marie couldn't wait to look through it, taking her time to see each photo and read every word. Fortunately, it was on a slow day, while she was at the registers, so she had to put it down a couple time to help customers check out. It took almost two months before I saw everyone, with Katie being the last to see it. I went into the store specifically to see her as I hadn't seen her for at least a couple months.

Everyone who looked through it was amazed. Associates tried to tell me the wonderful changes were all my doing; I still replied it was all due to them. They provided the ideas and guidance for how to improve my skin and become at least competent with many of the makeup products. October was the first time I'd ever worn eyeliner. After a month, no one believed it; they all said I did such a good job with my eyes. The few who refused to accept any credit said beauty advisors can only tell people how to apply and work with the different products, meaning the actual practice and routines were fully on me. I knew better than to disagree with them. I let the topic go while knowing I was right: my growth was Sephora's fault.

While I made many friends between the stores, I was still trying to navigate how to talk with other women. It was never a strong suit in my youth, and now that I'd transitioned, I sensed different parameters of conversing as a woman with other women. When you haven't grown up in circles of female friends, it's hard to know what makes appropriate conversation. I worried about how easy it could be to overstep boundaries without realizing it.

For transparency, I was never good at talking with men when I was pretending to be one of them, either. I never felt fully comfortable around most of them, and the things they discussed beyond work topics never quite interested me. I was more interested, more connected, with the topics I usually heard women discuss.

Those associates—friends—were great at helping me navigate such quandaries. The women who were easiest to talk with genuinely discussed a variety of topics with me. When someone opened up to me about more than just cosmetics, to tell me something about themselves or ask me more personal questions, I learned who might accept more indepth, friendship-level conversations. Some led with openness, like Wendy, who told me bras shouldn't be removed until the evening cleansing routine was complete. I figured out with which ladies I seemed to have common ground and shared interests. I learned who it was safe to mention being on HRT to, and who I could open up with when I was going through an unusual roller-coaster period, and just needed to let someone know.

While gender dysphoria is often discussed in regard to transgender individuals, it was something I tried not to think about most of my life. It was taxing enough to live in a body that felt incomplete and wrong. The features I saw in the mirror matched what the outside world— including my family—expected me to look like. Even though I was never happy with how I looked, it was possible to let it go... at least to some degree. Yet once I began to transition and start HRT, many of the features I'd been able to ignore were no longer so easy to overlook. The aspects that never felt right in my life began to fight back and bother me.

One night in early February, I looked in the mirror and felt whiskers on my face. They undid me. Those little things were identifying aspects of a body that refused to align with the female I was inside. Although the product I used to slow and stop hair growth on the face was making progress, just seeing the small whiskers, feeling them with my hand, started a waterfall of tears, followed by a cascade of sadness. I couldn't stop thinking about other aspects of maleness that remained hidden or that I'd ignored in the past, yet were now surfacing, asking for attention.

I needed to talk with a friend, someone I could trust would be there to listen. I knew I tended to pull back from others when I felt alone and insecure. That night, I was sure there was no one I could speak with about going through a tough time. As I fell asleep, I prayed for help to overcome fears and tears.

The next day, trying to put the tears behind me, I went to Sephora. Inside the store, I saw three friends who I thought I could tell of my hard time, and maybe even share my concern about pulling away from others. Even though many associates have become friends, unless I have specific product questions, I'm always conscious of talking with them when the store gets busy. Fortunately, the day remained on the quiet side.

I spoke to Betsy first, telling her about my emotional roller coaster while touching briefly on some of the issues bothering me. From the beginning, Betsy talked openly with me, much like how I imagined an older sister might. I let her know how I reacted to such waves in the past, pulling away from the people who meant the most to me because I was never sure who was safe. Her response was cheerful. She said it was good I recognized the ways I reacted in those situations, and I was taking the right steps.

Julie was next. She was always such a positive lady to be around. While mentioning being up and down, I also expressed how I lacked friends to confide in. As the store was quiet at that moment, she had time to listen. It was like a cooling salve on a burn, as if all I needed to feel better was to have someone listen. Yet the real healing of our conversation came when we spoke of the impending cold weather. I loved cooler temperatures, having grown up in northern Maine. When she asked how I ended up here, I told her about the three places my parents considered moving to when I entered high school. Her response was priceless, making my day: "I'm glad you moved here!"

Then there was Marie. She was working in one of the aisles when I said hi. She asked how I was doing, which she often did when there was a chance to talk. I told her about my ups and downs and some of the reasons behind the emotional roller coaster. There was an opportunity for us to chat just a minute or two, which was often all the time I had with anyone. With Marie, her tone and what she said relaxed my nerves. Though she didn't know it, that day wasn't the first time she's helped me feel better through an innocent chat. In fact, the following week, when she saw me in the store, Marie pulled me aside and asked, "How are you doing... how are you really doing?" I couldn't remember anyone doing something like that for me before. I loved her positive energy!

On the days when I felt low or had a transition-influenced emotional roller coaster, I was amazed at how everything calmed down when I visited Sephora. My wellbeing significantly improved once I stepped through the store's entrance. The beauty advisors always had a way to brighten my day, whether they knew I was down or not. Those who knew I might be having a rough time often checked in with me when they saw me. I've tried to be available to lift them up, too, which is why so many in Sephora feel like family.

The ladies in MAC and Sephora were always happy to see me, and I them. And the person I saw least frequently often provided the most eye-opening comments. Heather consistently caught me off guard in a positive fashion. The second time I saw her in February, Heather's words threw me for a loop.

27

And Then There Was Heather...
Part 2

Heather has always been positive, both around and about me. Heather is a person who sees the best in people and only wants to help them fly. That's what this butterfly loves so much about her!

I saw Heather again at my Sephora store one week after seeing her at the new store opening in February. She'd told me the previous week that she'd be stopping by that day, so I looked forward to seeing her and finally showing her "The Book." When she arrived, she was immediately busy with the associates. She knew everyone! Still, when she saw me, she took a few minutes to talk and look through the photo book. Like everyone else, she was amazed at how much I changed over the year. It had been less than four months since we first met.

We didn't talk much beyond that, and I left to make a couple more stops in the mall before heading home. However, on my way to the car, I passed Sephora again and saw her inside. Something told me to get in line to enter. When I reached the front of the line, she was by the entrance. Inside, we had our first truly focused conversation, where it was an open time to talk as if we were meeting at a coffee shop to catch up with each other.

In that conversation, Heather made clear she's always seen me as just another woman, and that she couldn't see me as anything other than how I presented myself. When I showed her my driver's license photo, which was taken four years ago, and a photo of me that day without my mask, she couldn't believe the difference. Even though she knew my journey, Heather said from the first time she saw me, I've only been Susannah to her.

"One area that I'm always fearful will 'give me away' is my voice," I told her. "Yet hearing you and many of other ladies in the store recently tell me that my voice is fine was critical to lowering my nerves on that subject."

"Think about the people you've met recently," she said. "Do you think any of them thought you were anything other than the woman you present?"

I had to admit everyone, including Amy, one of the ladies I met the previous week at the store opening, treated me as any other woman. She was working in Macy's the day I chatted with Heather. Amy's at least as tall as me, and when I went over to where she was working, we talked for a few minutes. The conversation felt like two ladies beginning a new friendship. During my chat with Amy, part of me wanted to ask her if she could tell I was trans, although I knew to just watch my words and enjoy a budding friendship.

"I'm finding that I need to think about what I say in front of new people," I told Heather. "I do realize they see me the way I present myself, although the person they visually see is only six months old. My look and full use of makeup only began at the end of August, while I'll complete eight months of HRT in a couple days. This means I have to consider my words carefully if asked about my past with anyone who doesn't know my full background."

OK, let's face it: I can't say I was a US Army Cavalry Officer without raising questions, since women were not in combat arms branches when I served. If I mention being married, that also becomes difficult to explain since my transition occurred during my marriage. I find the best approach is to avoid such subjects as much as possible, only opening up to people I have known and trusted a while.

Heather mentioned a Sephora program called "We Belong to Something Beautiful," where both Sephora staff and customers do short video presentations. Not only did she offer to send me a link to look at the videos, Heather suggested I consider doing a video. She also said she could introduce me to those who were putting them together. While the thought of doing a video sounded exciting, it would also be a huge step further out of that closet and into the public eye. It was something I needed to think over and pray about before making a commitment.

As we talked, I mentioned how I felt blessed this transition was happening the way it was, including the realization of being glad God didn't answer my three-year-old self's prayer to wake up as a girl. I wouldn't be the person I am now, which means I'd miss out on being a cavalry officer and wouldn't have met the wonderful people who now grace my life and have been so supportive.

Had my prayer been answered, I'd be different. My style, life, friends, and experiences would be different from who I am... and I'm finally liking and gaining confidence in me! God has a plan, and while I can pray, He knows exactly what I need.

Heather and I are close in age and could be sisters. Before I left, Heather initiated doing an elbow bump saying, "It will have to do for now until we can actually hug." It surprised me, leaving a warm feeling inside.

After that last visit with Heather, I mulled over how, during the past six months, my focus was on properly presenting myself to the world as a woman, as Susannah, while simultaneously erasing decades of "male" behaviors that aligned with my body. For so long, I had to walk, talk, and act like a man in this world. I played baseball, was in the military, worked with my dad, joined a men's Bible study group, and even went to a few men's church retreats. Yet for all those activities over the decades of my life, there was never a real desire or passion in me to be a man. There was nothing in me that wanted to be like the men around me. Even with all the testosterone that flowed through my body, it wasn't me, the real me. The conflict between who I really was compared to what others thought I was, put me in a difficult position. It required guidance. I constantly took my queries about self and direction to the Lord in prayer.

By the end of February, I was resolved to move forward to whatever the Lord had planned for my next steps. My prayers began to center on storytelling, where my passion lies. That includes writing my own stories across multiple genres and medias. It may include working with trans youth, who are often too young to stand up for themselves, yet not too young to learn how to tell their own stories, be they personal or fictional. It might be something I haven't yet considered but will be put on my heart. The world is finally open to me again, a place I can begin to fly with many different opportunities.

28

The Butterfly Effect

W hen I consider my journey to get to where I am today, I think often about the concept of the butterfly effect. The basic premise is, if something were to change in the past, no matter how slight, it can have a profound consequence on future events. Whether it happened thousands of years ago or during a person's early childhood, no matter when, the result would impact the present day. I first learned about the idea when reading Ray Bradbury's time-travel short story, "A Sound of Thunder."

In my case, if my prayer had been answered at age three and I woke up one morning a girl, from that point forward everything in my life would be different than the life I've lived. Growing up being recognized and treated as the girl I am would have made me an entirely different woman than I am today.

Each person's life is unique. How I grew up and lived made me the woman I am today. Because I grew up in a male body, I accomplished things that weren't possible for other women, like my time serving in the Army as a cavalry officer. My lived experiences impacted who I am now, what knowledge I had going into transition, and what I needed to learn from the women who became my closest friends during that transition.

If I woke up as a girl at age three, my experiences would be unlike what they were on the path I lived. Living life as the woman I am from age three would shape me into someone I wouldn't recognize. We are the sum of our experiences, so it's possible that had He answered that prayer, I would not have the relationship with the Lord I have now. My connection to Him was critical to helping me finally feel right about who I am and where I'm going through transition.

If that prayer had been answered, I wouldn't have met the many supportive people who entered my life over the past couple of years, people I dearly love.

Looking back, there are many points where it would be easy to say, "If only I had done _____." However, I'm glad do-overs are not possible. To change something, maybe come out sooner or stand up for myself in childhood, would enact the butterfly effect. Whatever revisions I might consider making to my past would cause reverberations in my life that would fundamentally change the person I am now. I would not have the wonderful friends I've made since emerging from my closet. It's even possible I could have turned out to be a person I dislike. I know my history and the events which led to this point, how I've been locked away in hiding. Those years were difficult, filled with fear—especially fear of people who look at the surface of a person rather than the heart. I finally have the courage to stand up, move past my fears, and exit my closet. The result is having many friends whose hearts are good, who genuinely tell me they enjoy seeing me. For the first time I feel loved by people outside my family, and it's truly wonderful!

I'm finally happy about the person I've become and have no desire to lose the friendships I've made, especially at Sephora and MAC. Through transitioning and HRT, I finally like the person I am. Looking in the mirror, even though I often see the "past" me trying to peek out, the lady I see in my reflection is happy. She's starting to truly enjoy life in ways she was missing since her early childhood!

Though it took a long time, I can finally look in the mirror and say, "I love who I am."

At the end of 2019, it was virtually impossible for me to say those words. In 2020, they became more believable. In 2021, I can say them, even when I consider how to approach my family about who I really am, a woman beginning to blossom.

29

A Bittersweet Spring

There is always a sense of renewal and growth in springtime. Leaves begin to bud on the trees, and flowers start to show themselves as the weather warms up. Yet this year, March and April provided a period of bittersweet memories. Many of the beauty advisors I viewed as close friends were leaving to start new chapters in their own lives. They left for new beginnings, while for me, it was a time to say goodbye and let them know how much I appreciated them in my life. While saying goodbye was difficult, there were special moments that I will cherish the rest of my life.

Parting with friends was difficult for me. Half a dozen advisors left the store for new opportunities, including some moving into totally different industries. While they were all important to me, the one I was closest with was Laura. She was the one who first told me she wished she could give me a hug after my mom passed away. She was there to talk with about anything: makeup, skincare, or how I was feeling. She gave me makeup advice when I showed her my photos. It was Laura who was in the "Grinch" photos with me at Christmas, and Laura who suggested I get a red mascara to accentuate my blue eyes.

Twice, when I was having a tough time, Laura told me she wanted to give me a hug. On her last day, she made up for those lost opportunities by giving me three hugs! We each said we'd miss seeing one another in the store. She was one of the few ladies I spoke to about more than just cosmetics. She would tell me how she was doing, and talk about her family, and I would be there to listen and support. She did the same for me. On that last day, I showed her a recent photo of my face after cleaning, and beside it, one from 2019. She saw the vast improvement between them, and it felt good to have a friend with whom I could share.

Vanessa also left. Though we didn't talk as much, she was always in my corner when I was in the store. She observed what I wore, commented when she saw something she thought was special—like my blue turtle-neck-sweater dress and over-the-knee black boots, and she was the associate to whom Joy referred to me as "she" for the first time. In March, before she left, we had a chance to talk, and Vanessa said everyone liked when I visited. Usually, they felt like glorified bouncers trying to keep people from sampling products due to COVID restrictions. I told her I was starting to write a memoir of my transition. As we talked, she suggested I do the Sephora "We Belong" video. I said Heather suggested the same thing, but I wasn't quite ready for such a public step of coming out. Still, the seeds were planted.

Though some friends left, I still had many who watched me grow, along with some new beauty advisors who'd recently begun working in the store. Cheyenne was one of the ladies who I recognized from before shutdown, and finally began to talk with in November. By springtime, I realized we could talk about almost anything, having several common interests between us. It was Cheyenne who introduced me to boots, and somehow, I ended up with one or two pairs that she had. We also talked cooking, my background, and her background, and she helped me pick out some beautiful eyeshadows.

Julie was another with whom I was getting close. I told her about upping my estrogen for HRT in February. One day in March, out of the blue, she quietly asked me if I was feeling anything from the upped dosage. I could have hugged her, as asking the question conveyed a sisterly love I rarely experienced. I told her I hadn't really noticed any changes with the increased dose, and how I took monthly measurements since beginning HRT to track my changes thus far... besides my weight.

Conversations with Julie revealed how close we were becoming as friends; they also confirmed what others told me. In one instance, Julie apologized when she had to help a customer. I was used to hearing that from other beauty advisors as well. I said it was always fine with me when that happened since that's what she was there to do. However, her next words caught me completely off guard.

"You're also a customer," she said looking at me. Then, after a slight pause, Julie followed that up with, "No, you're actually more like family."

That simple statement brought such loving tears to my eyes. I don't think any of my friends in Sephora, the ones who supported me and watched me emerge from my own cocoon-of-a-closet, will ever know how important they've been in helping me heal from years of pain and abuse.

On my birthday, Julie's words truly hit home. When I arrived that day, Debbie announced through her earphone that I was about to enter the store. Although I didn't recall anyone doing that before, I didn't think too much about it. Inside, I saw Katie and went straight to where she was to ask her about some products. Not long after we started talking, Betsy came up behind me with a small pot of planted yellow tulips, a small birthday balloon, and two cards. Not only did they know it was my birthday, it became the best birthday I could remember! As I walked around the store, beauty advisors came over to wish me a happy birthday. It was the first time I remembered feeling important to anyone outside my wife and daughters.

When I got home, I cleaned off the table to set up my flowers, balloon, and cards. I waited to get home to read the cards as it was likely I'd start crying in the store if I read them there. There were so many beautiful comments from different beauty advisors and associates, and it made my day to know there were people in my life who truly cared about and loved me for who I was, the real me. I made sure to provide a "thank you" comment to everyone after my visit.

~~~~~~

Actual Sephora survey comments from my store visit after my birthday:

[It] was my birthday, and even though I was in the middle of a virtual writer's conference, it was important to me to visit Sephora on that day to spend at least a part of my birthday with my friends / family who have helped me to grow in so many ways and been so support-ive of me this past year—I love them all so much! What was not expected was to receive flowers and cards signed by the associates after entering the store! (I've read those cards multiple times every day.) As I browsed through the store, everyone who saw me came over to wish me a happy birthday. <3

It was good that I waited to get home to read the cards, as the reality of the love from everyone that filled them hit me after reading the beautiful sentiments that were written, and my tears began to flow. My Sephora family made this birthday the best that I can remember. I truly wish it were possible to give every one of them a huge hug... they've added so much positive energy and joy to my day—and life.

~~~~~~

I had an amazing family at the mall. There were ladies in different stores I could talk to, ask questions of, and interact with on almost a family level. I knew they truly supported and cared about me from their comments and the smiles I saw in their eyes. They were people with whom I finally felt safe to be around.

30

Family Events Are Not Easy for Me

My niece's graduation party was fast approaching. Primarily a family event, it was the first time I'd see my dad and brothers with their families since Mom died. It was also near the end of my first year of HRT.

Fortunately, I had a couple months to prepare for the actual party. Once on my radar, my first thought was to see how much I'd changed since August. When I compared photos from the graveside service with current ones, the changes were obvious, including significant variations in my facial structure and skin. I liked how I looked, so it was difficult to consider what to do and how far to tone down my appearance to align with the past.

I firmly believed coming out at the event was not right. It was important to me that I didn't take anything away from my niece's day. She was the center of attention. It was her day to shine for her accomplishments, and she justly deserved being everyone's focus that weekend. Conversely, if I came out before the party, there was still the possibility I would cut into her moment, especially if I was no longer allowed to attend after the reveal. It became a fine line between toning down my looks to align with the past and avoiding the complete erasure of my true identify while with family.

My friends at the cosmetics stores in the mall knew about the event. Let's face it, they were the only ones I could turn to for help and ideas about how to modify my look so as not to attract too much attention. However, I had also reached the point where I could no longer comfortably leave the house without first putting on at least basic skincare and makeup. At a minimum, I wore tinted moisturizer daily, though when going to the mall, my preference was for full coverage foundation. I wore basic eyeshadow shades, mascara, and black eyeliner. I enjoyed having a little blush on my now prominent cheeks. I wore lipstick beneath my mask and enjoyed wearing dangly earrings.

A month before the event, many of the beauty advisors began to ask me how it went. Though they didn't know the exact date, they were aware of how much I worried about my presentation. It was one thing to tell them about the party and my need to look similar to how I did in August when my family last saw me; it was another thing entirely to realize the associates remembered the party and were thoughtful enough to ask about it. Their questions told me they truly cared about how I felt after attending the event.

My biggest cosmetics concerns revolved around my eyes, lips, and nails. I always felt at my best with colorful eyeshadow, black eyeliner, and mascara. Spending time around family, however, required me to tone it down or eliminate eye makeup altogether. I talked with a half dozen beauty advisors about options, often asking about their eye makeup when I noticed they had beautiful neutral looks similar to my goal. Each time new options popped up, I tried them at home to see if they were truly what I sought. When I felt like I found the right combination, including a light brown mascara, I wore it to the store to get the approval of my friends. Hearing them say how good I looked, it was obvious my eyes were set.

My lips were another story. I enjoyed darker red and pink lipsticks, stains, and tinted balms, which added to my awareness of my feminine self. I loved adding beautiful colors to my lips to enhance the rest of my face. However, around family I wouldn't be in a mask, so I turned to lip balm options, looking for a light tint that still added a little color. I went around in circles with Wendy; the colors I liked kept coming out darker and more noticeable than she said was proper for the neutral look she knew I wanted to achieve. I would make my final decision the day of the party.

I intended to do my nails before leaving for the party. Since February, Anne did my nails every couple of weeks. One of my goals was to heal and strengthen my nails. She was fabulous! It only took a few weeks before I was ready to move from regular manicures to gels, which I loved even more! They were stronger, lasted longer, and still had a beautiful array of red and pink color choices to play with. Knowing I'd see her the day before leaving town, we talked about color options I could select from to "hide" my nail color while still having cute nails with the gel finish I enjoyed. There were some beautiful nude shades that would hide well on my fingertips. However, deep down, I wanted a light pink tint. It spoke volumes to me about knowing my true self and not covering up the emerging woman I was, so that's what I chose.

The day before the party, my daughter and I headed out of town, having booked a hotel near my brother's place. I stopped by the mall so I could get some positive energy before spending the next few days with family. It was exactly what this girl needed! Everyone I talked with wished me well on the trip, and Julie was adamant I tell her how I was doing both when I arrived and during the party. She said to be sure and let her know if I had any problems so she could send me a funny video to lift me up. It was the first time I remembered anyone asking me to keep in touch, much less instruct me to keep them posted on how I was doing and if I was having problems. In so many ways, it was an affirmation from above I was on the right path and with the right people... that I was loved.

The day of the party, I wore my favorite high-waisted women's jeans, a neutral light-blue t-shirt, and a darker-blue men's short-sleeved shirt that I left unbuttoned to better hide my curves. My makeup was light, requiring people to really look hard to see my eyeshadow and light brown mascara. The final touch was to tie my hair back in a ponytail, although I couldn't resist using a pink hairband.

After we arrived, I felt extremely uncomfortable and out of place, even with my toned-down look. It was a common emotion for me with my family, yet this time there was something almost ominous in the air. My dad, brothers, and their families were all present for the occasion. Deep inside, I needed to avoid interactions with others. I was starting to feel overwhelmed with worry about what they were thinking. My look was fluid between two genders. It didn't fall on one side of the imaginary line separating them. The ambiance felt stifling to me, so I went to a quiet area in the dining room to hide. I sent a text to Lauren letting her know how glad I was my youngest daughter was with me. I also made some notes for one of my stories. After a short while, my daughter came over to me to check in and make sure I was alright. I told her everything was fine and to go back and enjoy her time with her cousins. After spending so much positive time around everyone at Sephora and MAC, I'd forgotten how difficult it was for me to spend any amount of time with my own family.

At one point I went outside with my middle brother to give him his birthday presents. I came out to him as he put the gifts in his car. He was not surprised. When I asked him not to tell anyone, he was concerned about not talking with his wife, who was best friends with my ex. I promised I'd let my ex know soon.

Although I was sure everyone noticed my changes, no one said anything specific to me. I conversed with a couple people on more general topics, though I tried to keep brevity in my comments. I considered asking my brother if he heard anyone say anything about me, but the opportunity passed.

When we left my brother's place, I took off the men's shirt before getting in the car.

After entering the hotel room, I threw the shirt across the space towards my suitcase and enjoyed the rest of our trip as the real me.

After that event, I realized wearing men's shirts around family... or anyplace, for that matter, had negative effects me. It was like wearing a straitjacket. I felt restricted, unable to be myself or open up to people when talking with them. It created in me a need to hide, to stay away from everyone, leaving me extremely uncomfortable and out of place around people. As a woman, I'm free to talk with others and be me. Pretending to be male is confining, restraining, and removes any joy or desire to interact with others.

I had to stop pretending and finally be the woman I've always been... in public, not hidden in a dark closet. Yet one of my biggest fears revolved around my face. We approached a time when masks would no longer be necessary in public. It was my manicurist, of all people, who kept telling me all my fears were unfounded.

31

Tales of the Manicurist

Ever since Christmas 2019, I enjoyed keeping my nails painted. At first, I chose subdued shades that gave me a little color but kept them "hidden" from casual observers. There were a few times I went with a clear coat for a color break, though usually I only chose colorless nails if a family member was visiting. The pandemic and its subsequent need to stay home most of the time afforded me an opportunity to expand my color selection to brighter shades, deep reds, and lovely pinks. It was a simple way to express myself.

During the latter part of 2020, when stores were beginning to open, my color selection remained on the bolder side. I wore bright shades on my nails while shopping. The color helped me feel more like myself with each trip. Painted nails also helped me write. Seeing the colorful tips of my fingers tickle my computer's keypad strengthened my creativity.

Near the end of 2020, I mentioned to Sally that I was considering getting my very first manicure. She said she could give me the names of some manicurists when I was ready. The seed was planted. For the next month I nurtured it and let it grow, considering when I would take the plunge to get my first professional manicure. I returned to Sally for recommendations. When I mentioned needing help to improve the health of my nails, she knew exactly who I should call: Anne.

It still amazed me how easy it was to walk through the doors God opened for me through my transition. I contacted Anne, and she was able to quickly work me into her schedule for my first appointment. By early February, I was getting ready to enter a salon for my first ever manicure, and to meet someone who would only know me as Susannah. Anne had no hint of my background.

Due to COVID, upon arrival I had to call Anne to let her know I was there. She would then come to the front and open the door to let me in. Anne's salon was located within a larger space housing several individual hair and nail salons. Anne was shorter than me, with hair that was lighter blonde than mine. She had a cheery voice. With my mask, I felt less fearful of being outed during the appointment. Anne quickly put me at ease, and we chatted the entire time. The conversation felt natural, especially as she made comments with female-gender words which helped me realize I was in the right place as a woman talking with another woman. Over the next few months, our friendship developed and grew. Anne's manicures yielded beautiful outcomes and offered stimulating conversations. She was a new and amazing friend.

Anne was a huge positive in my transition, though it was also with Anne that I first realized I needed to be careful about what I said to people who didn't know I was trans. My life experiences were unique for a woman, and if I talked about doing something women didn't do, like being a cavalry officer in the Army, it could become awkward. If I became too comfortable, it was possible that I could inadvertently say something to "out" myself. I felt it was not proper to talk about things like my military background, wife, daughters, etc., if I wanted to avoid potentially uncomfortable questions.

I also realized that, unlike most coming out situations, my coming out flowed in two directions. For those who knew me before transition, I was coming out by letting people who thought of me as male know I was transitioning to my true female self. They were the ones who already knew my history. However, I was now making friends with people who only knew me as a woman, like Anne. While it might be nice to keep the relationships that way, there were times when it felt necessary to come out to them, too. In those cases, the situation was reversed: letting them know I was transgender and had a history which included living uncomfortably as a male for a half century.

As summer approached, two events eventually led to my coming out to Anne. The first was the planned family event for my niece. The second was the arrival of my youngest daughter. I wanted her help choosing a nail color for my niece's party. My daughter would likely be the tipping point to out myself. I was able to anticipate the question that would open the door for my coming out: "Does she live with your husband?" Fortunately, Anne also made it easier for me to come out to her, having a card on a bulletin board in her salon that noted being a friend for LGBTQ. Thus, when Anne did ask, my response was ready: "Actually, I've only been this way since last August."

Anne, bless her heart, said, "I had no idea. You look and sound like any other woman around here."

Since I came out at the start of the appointment, I spent the rest of the time talking about my background, finding more commonalities between us, and creating a stronger bond of friendship. I even showed her the photo book so she could see how much I'd changed since that first day with Joy. There was no difference in how she treated or interacted with me after I let her know I was a trans woman. If anything, she was even more supportive, helping me to know that, from an outside perspective, no one saw me as anyone other than another woman.

The best example of her verbal support came after the state removed the mask requirements. I needed to find someone to style and highlight my hair for the first time, and I asked Anne for names. At our first appointment without a mask, one of the stylists I was talking with (who was located in the same salon area), came into Anne's space and talked with me to both introduce herself and briefly discuss hair options. Before she left, we scheduled my very first hair-styling appointment. The experience confirmed what Anne kept telling me: I was only seen as a woman, nothing else. Later, when I told Anne how good it felt, she lovingly scolded me, telling me as she had so many times before—no one could tell, and all I had to do was confidently be myself.

Although she's my manicurist, she's also become one of my best friends. Her support and affirming manner helped me let the fears pass and just be me. Anne didn't care what I was, as she could tell I was being the woman I've always been.

32

My First Real Road Trip

With the difficulty of being around family for my niece's graduation party in the rearview mirror, the next day it was time to get on the road and head north. It was my very first road trip as my true self, accompanied by my daughter. She was awesome as we travelled, supporting me throughout the trip. From where my brother lived, our destination was only a couple hours away, yet there was a real sense of freedom in it. We headed to a town where I had scheduled three meetings to talk about writing and publishing. I was looking forward to each one with wonder and excitement. Best of all, masks were not required when outside buildings.

It was also the first road trip with my daughter in a couple years. On every visit we found time to travel, whether spending a few days at the beach or going camping. It was our time to see new places or revisit favorite sites. Time together was sparse due to distance and her school schedule.

Before leaving town, we went to a nearby Sephora. I noticed a strange tinge to my foundation when looking in the hotel mirror and wanted to verify what it was, as well as find a small moisturizer. It was my first visit to a Sephora store without a mask in over a year, and I was a little nervous. When we arrived, we seemed to be the only customers in the store. A beauty advisor greeted us as we entered, and she was a lot of fun to talk with. Just like my experience at home, she quickly put me at ease. I began with my foundation question, and she said it looked great to her. She brought me to a mirror so I could see for myself, and she was right. The tinge I saw was most likely created by the lights around the mirrors in the hotel. It was a joy to talk with her as we looked around the store. My daughter had fun as well, looking at different skincare and cosmetic products. We both agreed we wouldn't mind visiting the store again in the future.

The drive to our destination was uneventful, which was nice. We arrived in the early afternoon and took the opportunity to explore a little before checking into the hotel. We went to the bay to see what it was like, and my daughter took "in public" photos of me as I sat on a bench. I felt so much better than I had the previous few days with family. I was free, free to be me in the wide-open spaces by the bay. As we walked and passed by other people, it felt good to observe how no one gave us a second glance, no one stared. I was accepted for being me, which increased my confidence.

I had three meetings over two days, and the first two were with ladies who only knew me from an email asking to meet when I was in town. The last meeting included Claire, who I'd met three years earlier at a writer's conference in New York; she was also the fourth person I came out to. Going in with self-confidence led to meetings where I was open, asked questions, and began to make good connections with new people. It was also a chance to dress more business-like in a nice skirt and loose sweater top.

The first meeting was with a small press publisher. I learned about the organization from an online conference a few months earlier. I had two fantasy books ready to publish, and the option of self-publishing was intriguing. The first meeting was an opportunity to make sense of this type of publishing and learn what services they provided for new authors. We met in a bookstore, a great venue as it provided someplace for my daughter to hang out while we talked.

With the second meeting later in the afternoon, my daughter and I decided to visit a nearby beach park to see the water and take a few photos.

It was sunny with a few clouds, though not quite as warm as we might like. It was a good experience, though, to be outside on a beach that was more pebbles than sand. We walked to the water, watched others, and had a good time enjoying the fresh air. We also took photos before leaving for my next meeting.

The second meeting was with another author who had self-published. I was familiar with her from the same conference. She had a lot of success with her historical fiction novels. We met outside a store, and she talked about her different works and showed me some of the ways she marketed her books. Her creativity gave me ideas for promoting my own books when I reached the publishing stage. We were both historians with a background in Nordic and Norway-specific history, so it was fun to talk about our different interests in those fields. She was more focused on World War II underground history. While I had some knowledge of Norwegian underground activities, my real focus was on US-Nordic diplomatic history, especially in relation to the beginning of the Cold War.

The second day began with a quick drive to a nearby park that claimed to have four waterfalls. My daughter and I enjoyed hikes where we could walk fairly easy trails together and appreciate the scenery. For me, it was a chance to hike in a skort for the first time. As with all "firsts" I experienced during the previous year, I felt a new level of freedom as we walked along the trails. And it wasn't just because I wore a skort instead of pants. Everything around me felt more open and full of positive energy. The air seemed fresher, too. We had fun taking different trails and finding beautiful locations for both scenic and personal photos. It was a great way to relax before returning to the hotel to prepare for the last meeting.

Even though it was sunny, it was also fairly windy. I decided to wear my floral dress with ruffles and put my hair in a ponytail to keep it from blowing around. I was looking forward to seeing Claire. Prior to spending these days in her neck of the woods, I set up a video chat with her to open up about my transition. I didn't want it to be a surprise when I saw her in person. She was awesome as we chatted on the call, and I felt safe with her. Claire worked with Joyce, so it was also a chance to meet Joyce for the first time. While I'd seen her at a couple online writing conferences, she wouldn't know me. I used an older photo of myself during Zoom conferences, having registered under my old name.

We met in town, then walked to a small café. I walked with Claire, since I'd known her for a while, and my daughter walked with Joyce. It felt good to hear Claire's compliments on how I looked. I enjoyed spending time with the two of them, catching up with Claire while getting to know more about Joyce. It was also a chance to share parts of my own background and answer any of their questions. Both ladies were amazing, putting me at ease with a feeling of being welcome during the visit.

The return trip home was also positive. It took about six hours to get home, so we stopped around the halfway point to do some shopping. We checked out some discount stores, tried on clothes, and purchased some beautiful outfits. We also refueled our stomachs before heading home.

Throughout the entire trip, I was accepted for who I am. In the meetings and while walking around in public, I saw no scrutinizing looks and heard no negative comments about who I was or how I looked. I was treated as the woman I knew I was, gaining friends, acceptance, and confidence with every step.

33

Two Coming-Out Stories

A couple significant events occurred during the days leading up to my first birthday in HRT years. I came out to my ex, then to my dad.

My ex came to pick up my youngest daughter for a short trip they'd planned for the middle of the summer break. Since it was one of the hottest days of the year, and I was living full time as my true self, I met her wearing a tank top and skort, with my hair in a ponytail. I talked with my daughter first over a few days, just to be sure she was fine with what was about to happen. The short time with my ex was an odd case of coming out to someone. The topic—the huge elephant in the room—was never discussed. Instead, it was obvious I had come out based on how I dressed... did I mention my bright red nails? The entire time we were in each other's proximity, she said nothing about how I looked. It was only the usual superficial small talk. However, the atmosphere felt alright. I was worried about her reaction because I remembered how she was about my crossdressing during our marriage. She laid my fears to rest when she sent me a simple email a couple days later saying she was glad to see me living my truth. It turned out to be a positive experience with her.

Then, I came out to my dad a few days later... the day before my first HRT birthday. I wanted to see him as I felt it best to tell him in person. I was tired of hiding, tired of the menswear "straitjacket," tired of not being able to be myself around family. Even though it was an important step to take, I had an idea of what the outcome might be and set the bar very low before we talked. Still, it wan't low enough.

I went in with grace and love, praying for the right words to say to him. I was prepared for rejection. He'd tried to squash the girl out of me throughout my childhood and adult life, which was why I took so long to finally live as the woman I was now seeing in the mirror each day.

When I told him I was trans, I wasn't prepared for the amount of venom in his response. The poison went in deep, hitting me emotionally at unexpected times for many days. I was often reduced to tears for long periods of time while trying to understand how anyone could put that kind of negative passion behind their words: anger, hate, and bitterness flowed through every word he spoke.

It's so much better when we speak life to each other—to lift each other up—instead of hate.

I knew such negative conversations happened to other trans women all the time at all stages of their lives. I'd heard the stories about how they were rejected for being themselves. The words from family could do more damage than almost anything else. As bad as my experience had been, I suspect it was much less horrific than what many in the trans community experienced. It was rejection, all the same, and none of us deserve to be rejected. After hearing my dad's venom-filled words, I also had a better understanding of why so many other trans kids and women considere suicide—taking their lives in the face of such hateful situations. I believe my saving grace that day was my faith, which helped me remain calm in front of Dad.

He made comments and asked questions, most of which I have no desire to recant; there was nothing positive in his words. However, I can say that when I did respond, miraculously, it was with a calm voice. There were two specific comments worth noting, First, he said I could not show up at his place "dressed as a girl," though in many ways he was probably thinking I shouldn't show up as my true self around him, period. I didn't respond to his words. As for the second, I believe he had an argument prepared to retaliate against my expected answer. It felt like he held a loaded shotgun, cocked and ready to fire both barrels when he said, "I suppose you think God made a mistake." The anger and venom in his cold, calculated words was thick. My response was calm, simple, and direct: "God doesn't make mistakes." That was about the end of our talk. After that, I quietly went in and walked through his house to say goodbye before leaving it for the last time.

Dad did call later to offer to talk in person again to see if we could find some type of compromise. He said his main concern was that he didn't want any discord in the family. My impression was his desire was that the distance between us wouldn't create disharmony within the family. It was as if he couldn't accept his family being viewed as not being harmonious to others.

Although I said meeting was possible, I was not available for the next few days. The truth was, I no longer felt safe around him. I needed time to heal, time to talk with my closest friends and heal from their positive energy. I didn't leave my house for a few days as I never knew when his words would reenter my thoughts. Upon thinking of his words, their pain tore through me, and I broke down crying. I haven't seen him since, and it will be a long time before I could consider visiting him again.

The day after talking with Dad, I sent notes to my closest friends about my experience with him. Their responses confirmed I had real friends, and for one of the first times in my life, I had chosen the right people to open up to. Two of them were from out of state, and they were the first ladies I came out to. Their support was comprised of few words, yet they were words that helped my healing process: "YOU ARE BEAUTIFUL! and so worthy of being your authentic self!" and, "...continue carrying on as the brave, courageous, powerful woman that you are."

Three other women were from Sephora. I saw them on my store visits over two consecutive days. Not only were they friends, but they were also other women with whom I could openly talk about faith. I spoke with Wendy first. She was close to my age and had similar life experiences. When we talked, I told her more about Dad, and how I realized from the beginning that he may never accept me, and how I was able to forgive him for his words. Though forgiveness didn't remove all the pain and heartbreak, it helped me move forward more quickly than if I continued to hold onto negative emotions... it allowed me to heal.

When Julie saw me in the store, she immediately gave me a long, loving hug. A few days later, when I thought about it, I still teared up, realizing Julie's hug was something I never received before, yet was so important to my healing process. She didn't speak, she just hugged as though sharing my pain, and provided positive energy to help me heal. Then she let me talk about what happened, which was when Marie also joined us and listened to part of the conversation. I talked with both ladies that day and felt their caring energy as they listened and said heartfelt words.

Sometimes when we're in pain, we don't need words, just loving actions. A quiet, caring hug can be more impactful than any words to help a hurting heart.

I wish I could say that coming out was always a positive experience, that I was always accepted for who I am and not viewed only as what I was. It would be wonderful to say that my low expectations were vastly exceeded, and that there was no hate whatsoever. Yet, I can't. Dad's words hurt for many days.

However, that's not really the end. While it may be the end of one life-long relationship, it's not the end of my love for my dad. Although it will take me time to overcome the pain of what he said, I can still forgive him. I accepted him for who he was before talking with him. Though he can't accept me for being the woman I am, a lady finally emerging from her closet into the light of day, I still accept him as the person he is and has always been around me. Acceptance is a step in the healing process.

When I think of that pain, I'm reminded that of all the people I've come out to who knew my past, only one did not readily accept and support me. Then I think about the women at Sephora. They taught me about skincare and cosmetics, listened and comforted me as friends when I was on emotional roller coasters, and showed me the way out of my shell to become a more engaging and confident woman. They were put on my path to remind me that more people wish me well than want to bully me.

I no longer see myself struggling, hoping to emerge from a dark closet. Instead, that closet turned into a cocoon, allowing me to complete my transformation into the beautiful woman I've always been. Now, finally out as the girl I knew I was at the tender age of three, I know I can achieve anything as a woman. God opened the world to me with friends and love at every turn. I'm ready to fly.

34

A Summer of New Beginnings

With the pain of my father behind me, it was time to move forward into a new month and into my second year of HRT. I had the support I needed from people I could trust.

While I never truly expected to transition when I first stepped into Sephora eighteen months ago, it was always in my prayers. I knew being allowed to emerge from the shadows and be the woman who had hidden inside a shell for so long was not totally in my hands. As the passage of time tried to take its toll on me and discourage me, my faith remained strong. When the Lord began to open doors and allow me to take key steps in my transformation, I didn't complain that those first steps took longer than desired. Instead, I viewed it as my faith being aligned with the right time to move forward.

One of the best parts of July was going places without a mask. While I still felt some anxiety without a mask in public, friends and family told me no one could see me as anything other than a woman in the world. It was difficult to believe them when I could see pieces of my old face in the mirror. "If I can see it, everyone can see it," I mistakenly thought. Even when I believe I blend in with other women in public, I still worry as my subconscious looks for any sign of being read.

My daughter and I planned a road trip to the beach. We would be on the coast for three nights and visit some of our favorite places and restaurants. It had become an annual summer tradition for us, and often included a couple days of camping, though this year the thought of camping was far from either of our comfort zones. Instead, we chose a favorite hotel.

We didn't anticipate restaurants decreasing their hours. The first night we wanted pizza, yet our favorite place was filled with people, which meant it would be a long wait. There were long lines at the drive throughs of fast-food restaurants, as they were not allowing customers inside. The slim pickings meant we had to pre-plan our meals, budgeting time to place orders and pick them up. The first night we had chicken and jo-jo potatoes from a grocery store. Though an unexpected meal option, it turned out to be a great choice. We took it back to the hotel and ate while watching a movie. Thus, each night became takeout plus a movie in the hotel.

What a life!

Even though it was summer, the beach was extremely cold. We needed layers of clothing even in the bright sun. The winds rolled through at over fifteen miles per hour bringing a significant chill with them. Yet, it didn't stop us from walking along the beach and enjoying ourselves and the beautiful ocean view. We found a few tidepools to watch and saw beautiful waves where the water was a clear, deep green as the sun shone through them. We enjoyed going near the water, then running backwards to keep our feet dry as the tide rolled onto the beach. Even though it was too cold to stop in one place to read, write, and observe our surroundings, it was still an amazing time in the great outdoors with my daughter, and that's all I could really ask for that summer.

July was also the first time I had my hair styled. From April 2017 to July 2021, no one cut my hair as I let it grow. It looked a bit shoddy those first couple years, yet I wanted long hair, and my wife supported my not getting it cut. My dad made curt comments about how it looked, saying no one would hire me looking so shabby. I was learning to stop letting his negativity affect me. In Sephora, for quite a while, many of my friends were suggesting I get my hair styled, yet I refused to do anything without Sally's permission. I leaned on her to help me become better at taking care of my hair, and to make sure my scalp was healthy before going for any type of treatment. As with my nails, I wouldn't style or highlight my hair until it was in good health.

When Sally agreed the time was right, I asked Anne for some names, since she knew the hairdressers around her nail salon. She also knew what my hair was like, so she made the initial contacts for me. She gave me a couple names, and after reaching out to them, I leaned towards Maeve. When Maeve met me during one of my manicure appointments, I immediately liked her, and we set up my appointment as we talked. After Maeve returned to her studio, I told Anne it felt good to be accepted as myself.

"You've got to stop worrying, Susannah," she said. "No one can tell. It's all in your mind."

I knew she was right, yet when I sat down in the chair for my first hair styling with Maeve, I looked in the mirror and saw my old face staring back at me. I felt a slight panic creep over me at the sight. Fortunately, Maeve put me at ease as we talked about highlights and how much to cut. Looking in the mirror again, the old visage was gone, and I relaxed, leaving my hair to her capable hands. I left it up to Maeve to decide how far to go with my highlights.

Maeve was a talker, like Anne. It was great for me, leading to wonderful conversations covering many subjects the entire time I was with her. She knew it was my first time with a hair stylist, though she couldn't believe I had never had it styled before. It was while she shampooed my hair that I let her know I was trans. We were talking about my daughter, and she asked, "Does she stay with your husband?"

I felt comfortable with Maeve, so I said to her, "I've only had this face since last August."

There was an almost imperceptible pause in the conversation before she stopped what she was doing to look at me and say, "I had no idea."

I smiled as we continued to talk about my background and how I got to this point. She was open and safe to talk with, never affecting how I felt with her before or after I came out. It felt good to not worry about what I can or can't say without accidentally "outing" myself. Instead, it was just two ladies talking about their backgrounds, common interests, and getting to know each other during their first hair appointment.

Before she started, Maeve took photos of my hair from the back, for a "before" picture. When she was done, she took the "after" pictures, and sent both sets to me. The first thing I noticed in the before pictures was how long my hair was before she started to trim it… much longer than I realized. The second thing I noticed was how my hair had a distinct darker red tone to it, something I never expected. My mom always wished she'd been a redhead like her dad, yet it seems I got the red hair, not her. When comparing the before and after shots, not only was my hair much lighter and wavier, but the shorter length was also beautifully highlighted with soft curls.

My daughter loved the new look! We took additional photos after I got home, especially as I knew my hair skills were not ready to duplicate Maeve's beautiful styling. Seeing the new me with a new hairstyle, including highlights and waves, felt invigorating. I looked at the photos and realized my conversation with Dad had made this step much easier to take. He told me I couldn't show up to his place as a girl. His refusal to acknowledge that I am a woman was his loss, and having my hair done by such a wonderful lady was exactly what I needed to finally cut the negative bonds and energy Dad had heaped on me for much of my life.

In July I got a new Primary Care Provider (PCP). I had a medical professional to oversee my HRT, and I needed a PCP to walk with me and help plan the necessary steps to maintain my overall health. The doctors I had seen rarely focused on my overall care. Instead, they discussed the reason for the appointment and then finished quickly instead of getting to know me and my holistic medical needs. Once my transition began, I no longer felt comfortable with the male doctors at my clinic. It was time for a new PCP, someone I felt safe being transparent with, who would be happy to accompany my journey of transition. I met my new physician, and within minutes, I felt safe with her and was glad to finally have a provider who felt like she actually cared about my medical background and wanted to set a plan to keep me healthy.

To close out the month, my daughter and I took a day trip to the beach. Even though it was as cold as our beach trip earlier in the month, it was a great way to spend one of our last summer days together. The day started off cloudy and cold, with the wind whipping off the ocean. It was nice to see the clouds dissipate as we arrived at the beach. We scheduled our time so we could be at the front door of our favorite restaurant when they opened. Inside, the tables were spread out to leave plenty of room between customers. Although there was additional seating outside, we chose to stay inside where it was warmer. I had a bowl of my favorite clam chowder with a side of cheese bread, while my daughter opted for fish and chips with a cup of chowder. Apart from the previous beach trip that month, we hadn't had our favorite seafood in almost two years. Afterwards, we walked along the cold beach, looked at tidepools, and took pictures of the ocean and various rock formations between the beach and water.

Being together on such a beautiful day kept my mind off the fact that my daughter would soon leave. It would be almost five months until I could hug her again. At least it was better than the eighteen months between 2019 and June when her visits kept getting postponed due to the pandemic.

On the day she left, we arrived at the airport about three hours before her flight. As she was a minor, I got a pass to go through security to wait with her until her flight departed. Time at the gate became one of our cherished traditions. We had favorite restaurants in the concourse area, usually a pizza place, and had time to relax and talk before it was time for her to board. It was always difficult for me to say goodbye at the airport. I'd watch her go through the gate door, then wait for her plane to leave. She's my baby, and I wish we had more time together over the years.

When she left, the summer felt over. There was no longer anyone else at home to make dinner and watch movies with. It was just me, contemplating what was next. That period of meditation led to some important decisions regarding my next steps.

35

The August Decision

At the start of August, I realized I'd been walking the fence between my past and who I've always been, for too long. Moving forward in life was difficult. In many ways, while looking for new opportunities to write and consult, I was still trying to identify as someone I wasn't. My reflection no longer looked like the person of old, instead looking more and more like the real me.

It was time to get off the fence.

Those were simple words to say, yet much harder to act upon. Getting off the fence meant letting strangers and HR people know my background. It meant opening myself up to connections from my past, letting them know I was a trans woman and hoping they would still be willing to talk with me. Thus far, I had only come out to four people from my past. True, the support from them was amazing. Yet there was no guarantee others would react the same.

My dad's reaction still weighed on me, and soon was followed by my youngest brother. At the end of the first week of August, I contacted him, knowing my dad had already outed me to him. It was one of the only times I didn't mind being outed by someone else. It would make it a bit easier to talk with my brother, as he and my dad were very similar. Shortly into the conversation, he took aim at me.

"I couldn't sleep for a week after my daughter's graduation party because I was worried about you." That was followed by him speaking of gender roles and the Bible, and a comment of how our mom wouldn't approve. While he talked, I didn't focus on his exact words or their tone. It allowed me to get through the conversation in better shape than I had with my dad.

I suspected my appearance at the party wasn't as neutral as I thought. His words confirmed it.

"I still focus on God, going to Him before taking any steps," I responded. "Plus, I've known this is who I am since age three."

There was a pause, and I suspected my words caught him off guard. I redirected the conversation to him and how he was a good father to his kids. My brother said it was enough to know I was a trans woman. He didn't want to see me as I really am, which was fine with me. People are at different stages, and to push too hard often leads to disastrous results. This was our first conversation on the subject, so it wasn't time for me to push anything. Overall, we talked for about fifteen minutes.

After the conversation, I realized he tried to guilt me by saying he was worried and couldn't sleep. Those words imply it was my fault he lost sleep, because he couldn't handle who I am. Whether that interpretation was true or not, deliberate or unintentional, I was learning to let such interactions pass through me instead of getting stuck inside where they could gnaw at my emotional wellbeing.

I was ready to move forward with life, while it felt like my father and brother were trying to use guilt to pull me backwards. They would only be comfortable around me if I identified as something I never truly was— nor could ever be. I realized I no longer needed to listen to them, or to follow my father's principles so that I can live the life God planned for me. While I may have begun to grasp that decades ago, it took this long to sink in. Though there was wisdom in much of what my parents had said in my life, many of their beliefs and ideals were not what was best for me. I struggled because I feared standing up to my father, only finding the strength to do so over the past few years.

Shortly after the conversation with my brother, I began to selectively look for people to come out to, individuals I didn't have a strong relationship with, yet who I liked based on prior interactions. I chose three people from a company I'd worked for a decade ago, each of whom I had very few conversations with back then. Two of them were currently at companies with posted positions that interested me. They were people I had no contact with since leaving the organization. I took time to craft my initial messages, editing over and over, trying to put the words together to hint at my changes without immediately coming out. I sent each message as my old self. Each person responded with a positive hello, opening the door for me to be transparent about being a trans woman.

First, I reached out to Jordan, a former HR person who always seemed kind, even though we never had conversations of any depth or length beyond an HR focus. I knew a bit of his background, which was why I felt safest reaching out to him first. In his reply, I could hear his voice from so long ago. His words were heartfelt, affirming I had taken the next positive step forward in my journey. By the end of the month, we met at a coffee shop.

It was an amazing meeting for me. It was my very first time seeing someone from my distant past in person. After parking, I saw him walking to our rendezvous location. Wearing a skort and blouse, I got out of my car, calling his name. As he looked at me, he smiled and said I looked great. Those simple words meant so much to me that day. It was wonderful to reconnect and catch up. As we talked, he offered to connect me with a couple people he knew, as I was looking for new freelance opportunities to write and tell stories. Jordan kept me at ease as we talked, even telling me he wanted to stay in contact on this new journey I was on. It was only my first month off the fence, and it felt good to sense my wings opening.

Being able to connect with people from my past in such a positive fashion was like a healing salve, especially after the sour conversations with family members.

36

August Pain

People will say they love and support you, even when going through a transition like mine. It creates a positive feeling of being loved, believing other people to be safe and trustworthy. Because of their affirmations, you believe you can lean on them and be honest with them about how you're doing and what's happening in your life.

There are times, however, when the people who say you can count on them and be genuine with your feelings can turn out to be the ones who hurt you the most, even if unintentionally. Going through transition is emotional enough, so being able to count on the people closest to me for support was vital.

Towards the latter part of August, someone I felt close to ignored my words and how I felt. I will call that person "Terry." Terry had an open invitation to stay in my house since they were in town for a few weeks. As they were close to me, I was happy to support them during their brief time in town. When they asked me if a guy I didn't know could also stay in my home, I responded, "I don't know this person and, in all honesty, strange men make me very uncomfortable... I don't feel safe right now if for any reason I am alone in the house with strangers."

It seemed simple enough. Maybe I should have said no straight up, yet Terry was important to me, and I didn't want to sound cold. Terry's request was also made on the anniversary of my mom's death, so it was already a tough time for me at home.

A couple days later, Terry stopped by the house to give me some flowers since I was still thinking about my mom. It was a beautiful gesture. Then they proceeded to tell me how the man they wanted to have in my home was bi and came out to his parents.

I couldn't understand what that had to do with the fact that I was uncomfortable around men. Why was such background information supposed to make me feel better?

The subject was dropped until the next evening. Then, Terry asked again, via text message, to let a male stranger stay in my house, even though I made it clear how uncomfortable that made me feel. Terry recapped their previous comments, and added, "He's also dated trans people and is a very good listener & support & resource!"

I fell to my knees as I read the message. I had been saying no, and Terry kept pushing back to get me to say yes. It was also obvious from the last note that Terry had outed me to a complete stranger. I felt violated, torn apart. I curled up in a protective ball on the floor, sobbing uncontrollably. I was alone in the house, and fearful that no one cared about how I felt, only what they could get from me. It was the deepest pain I'd ever felt in my life, more so, even, than the venomous words from my dad.

When I regained my composure, I told Terry their comments about the guy increased my sense of feeling threatened. I did not feel any safer about him. Then I wrote, "However, what I'm most concerned about is that you told him about me, you outed me, and I've been in tears from the moment I realized that." I said I needed to be alone, and it wasn't a good idea for Terry's friend to be in the house.

Terry's response came the next day. "Sorry to hear this," they began, saying they were only trying to help me, knowing I was going through a hard time due to the anniversary of my mom's passing. They didn't deny outing me.

I was fortunate to be able to contact my oldest daughter about the situation. I sent her a text, letting her know I was having a very emotional time. I told her she was one of the few people with whom I felt any sense of trust at the moment. She responded, "Of course you can talk to me about it."

I told her what was happening with Terry. She was very supportive. She wrote, "For the record, it is very valid that you would feel uncomfortable around strange men." She told me both she and her wife had my back.

That night I locked my bedroom door when I went to bed just in case Terry came into my house with the stranger, as they had a key. I fell asleep curled up in bed, shaking and crying. I couldn't remember doing that before.

The next day I shared Terry's response with my daughter. "That's not an apology," she wrote, and "Very patronizing." My boundaries were not being respected.

I told my daughter I felt violated that Terry wouldn't accept that "No means no." I told her stories I'd heard of women being pressured to do something they didn't want to do. Then, when they finally caved into the pressure, they felt guilty as though what happened was their fault. I told my daughter that was how I was feeling. I kept saying no, and Terry kept giving me reasons to go against what felt safe. When I think about what happened, I find myself curled up in a small ball, hugging my arms tightly wherever I am: in a chair; standing by a wall; in bed; and on the stairs. It was giving me a headache.

Knowing my daughter had my back made the pain easier to deal with. She said it made sense I felt that way. She offered to talk with Terry, though I asked her to hold off as I cared about Terry and knew they were in the middle of an important project. I could deal with my pain for now, knowing I had family support.

Despite the pain Terry unintentionally caused me, I forgave them in my heart. Just as with my dad, I knew the deliberate act of forgiveness would help me heal quicker than if I held onto the pain. Too often when we get hurt, the other person goes on with their life as though nothing happened. Meanwhile, we live with a pain sinking into our heart, holding us back from living life to its fullest.

My daughter wasn't the only one who validated my feelings about what happened. The second person I came out to mirrored my daughter's reaction when I told her. We had a chance to catch up shortly after those events transpired, and she validated my sense of being violated. The ladies

I told this story to at Sephora also supported and confirmed my feelings. It really helped to know who's in my corner, who supports me, and who I can turn to when I need an ear to bend. Having friends like that makes it much easier to go through such emotional events and to put them in the rearview mirror.

Even with support from friends, it was difficult to get over what happened. There were events happening that refused to let the pain die away, fanning the flames to keep the pain alive. I was honest with Terry about how I cried continually after the text about their friend having dated trans people. I told them it kept me from going out of my own home because I didn't want to break down in tears in public.

Terry's response felt more like a slap in the face. "I'm sorry you're hurting, but it might be worth examining where the fear is coming from and recognizing who is here to support you and who is here to reject you. I love you and would never expose you to anything or anyone that would jeopardize your growth. I hope you know that."

I knew where the fear was coming from: Terry's inability to accept that my "no" meant "no," not, "please keep feeding me unrelated reasons to ignore my personal sense of safety so I will ultimately do what you want me to do." The fear was real, not imagined. At that point in time, apart from three men: Jordan and two associates at Sephora, the only people I felt safe around were women. I did not feel safe around men ever since my dad began trying to purge the girl from my being.

I was able to sit down with Terry in early September to discuss the situation. I continued to be open and let them know how much I was hurt, and how it felt like they refused to listen to my worries and concerns, instead trying to get me to agree to something they wanted. Terry thought bringing the stranger into my life would be positive for me and would help me to feel safer around men. I was not ready for such a step. That I had always felt uncomfortable, to some degree, around men, never crossed their mind. It was a good talk to help us both move forward, even if only beginning with baby steps.

I learned someone who claims to be a supporter, an ally as I transition to live as the woman I've always been, can still cause untold damage when they fail to listen. It's a problem that can occur in any situation, the failure to listen and understand another person's point of view and concerns. August became one of the most painful months in my life because my deep fears and concerns weren't listened to. Yet, I also found love from those I hoped would be there to support me. I realized the Lord gave me a wonderful daughter and daughter-in-law, and amazing friends, people who willingly joined me on this journey and were there to support me. It was what I needed to rise from the depths of pain and begin to carve a new path in life.

37

ESSAY: Who Can I Trust?

Who Can I Trust?

A Personal Essay by Susannah Dawn

It's nigh impossible to navigate life without interacting with people, and how we do that is one of the things which makes each of us unique. Our ability to trust others plays a key role in how we relate to the people in our lives. From an early age, beginning with our parents, we develop a basic understanding of trust. As the world expands around us, we meet new people, develop friendships, and learn to go beyond the basic "surface" conversation to slowly open up about who we really are inside. While there are many levels of trust, closeness and superficiality often influence how much trust we'll have in someone.

What happens when we lose the ability to trust people? What if the ones who care for us and should be the safest people in our lives end up hurting us?

Trusting others became difficult for me at a young age and continued to be hard for over a half century. At too many key junctures of life, I felt various levels of fear and betrayal, impairing my ability to trust people. It led me to withdrawal, first from family, then friends, and the world in general.

My life wasn't always withdrawn, lived in the safety of my personal closet. My early years were full of fun, friends, and trust going into elementary school. I enjoyed running around and being free, being myself, no matter who was around. It was a time when the world lay open for me to explore.

My body told people I was a boy, even though it was clear to me from the age of three that I was really a girl. In the early grades of elementary school, my best friends were girls. However, once I began to exhibit feminine tendencies, the people I trusted, my own parents, became unsafe. I couldn't articulate why I knew I was a girl, primarily due to my age and fear of my dad. Yet once I felt rejected by family members, it became impossible for me to open up and tell anyone how I felt. I didn't talk about my dreams, fearing they'd be crushed as "wrong" and "unrealistic."

Dad's actions towards my girlish tendencies pushed me away. I was afraid to talk with him, and knew he'd discourage my dreams. He was all about practicality and financial gain, doing and learning what was necessary to get a well-paying job after school. If what I wanted to do wasn't practical or, in his view, financially successful, he was not sympathetic nor supportive. Instead, he was blunt, telling me how I was thinking about the wrong things and needed to shift my focus to something with realistic opportunities, a steady income, and a stable life.

With no positive input about my interests, and no acceptance of the real me, it became difficult to believe life could be fun. Dad never said he believed I would succeed at anything of interest to me. I liked playing baseball, even though the coach rarely put me in games. Dad never came to a game, nor asked about them. In high school, I had a strong interest in astronomy, and considered it as a career field. He didn't see it as practical.

It was hard to feel loved when I constantly hid from my dad. When I was teased on the school bus and called "Cinderella" by the other kids for carrying a paper sack with my schoolbooks "like a girl," I never told him. When I was bullied on the middle-school playground, I said nothing. I was afraid of my dad. There was no reason to believe any support would come from him.

Once I pulled away from family, distancing myself from friends became a natural and fairly easy thing to do. Since no one ever talked with me at school, it seemed no one really liked me anyway, though I never knew why. That silence confirmed there was no sense trying to make friends. Instead, I kept to myself through high school and college. I was unable to see signs of anyone liking me enough to want to be friends. Because of the experience with my family and school, it was safer to withdraw from and observe the world, to lessen the likelihood of getting hurt.

I'd been hurt by others many times. During my first marriage, my spouse's words often felt like knife nicks, little digs and cuts that weren't too awful in their own right, yet combined over fifteen years to feel like death by a thousand cuts. I lost faith in myself and trust in her. Early in the marriage she outed me to one of her friends for being a crossdresser. When she finally told me, it was framed in such a way that I believed I was a bad person if I didn't accept her reasoning and agree that she did what was right for her. She said she needed to share her situation with someone she could talk to, and obviously talking with me was not an option. It was also another example of how I didn't know how to stand up and take care of myself, instead trying to appease everyone else and avoid conflict.

Too often, I felt betrayed by the actions of others, which impaired my ability to trust people: my dad, who tried to spank and tease my true self into oblivion; my previous spouse, who outed me to their friend without my permission. Those are just two examples from a half century of feeling alone.

After I met my current wife, my ability to trust grew again. At the beginning of our marriage, there were times when she yelled when she got angry with me. Yet within her yells, I truly felt her love. I felt safer with her than I'd ever felt with anyone. There was finally one person in the world I could trust. She knew about me from the beginning and supported me to be myself. As my transition progressed, she always told me how great I looked. She not only saw my physical appearance, but she could also see my heart and how much better I was doing inside.

During transition, trust was as relevant and important as ever in my life. As a trans woman, living in a closet was constraining. Every aspect of myself had to stay hidden away. I was only allowed to come out when no one was home, which was soul crushing.

It was a day after Christmas when I met the first person, beyond my spouse, I felt I could trust, and she was in the most unlikely of places: Sephora. My focus was only on the products with no expectation to talk with anyone. I also didn't believe my appearance passed for a woman—at best I was androgynous, with shoulder-length hair and denim jeans. My goal was to find a foundation to practice with in the safety of my home. I couldn't have foreseen being helped by a beauty advisor who realized and accepted me for the woman I was as soon as she spoke with me. She was accepting and direct, asking questions to help her find the right products for me. She earned my trust by keeping me focused on her and cosmetics instead of letting my eyes wander the store to worry about what others might think. When she referred to me as "she" and "her" when talking about me with other associates, I slowly opened up and lowered my guard. I trusted her completely when she offered to remove the makeup she'd applied on my face, and I asked to leave it on. I walked in public with makeup on my face for the first time.

In Sephora, my trust in others not only began to grow; it seemed to grow exponentially. I was never pressured to come out of my shell any faster than I was comfortable. I was allowed to ask questions at my pace, to open up to different beauty advisors when I was ready. By the start of the holiday season, I realized everyone in the store knew me—even those I hadn't yet talked with. It was the first time I felt there were people in the world who really did like me and enjoyed seeing me, and that there was a place where I belonged.

Through the holidays and on into the next summer, visits to my friends in Sephora and another store allowed me to open up in ways I'd never been safe doing during the previous half century of my life. Always glad to answer my skincare and makeup questions, our connections deepened as we talked about ourselves as friends. It was a new experience for me. Everyone who knew about my transition said they not only saw the physical changes, but my growing confidence and poise showed through each time I visited. The Lord put the people I needed in my life, women I could trust who helped strengthen His armor for the times I would need it.

Towards the end of the fall months, there were people who would enter my life and lose my trust almost as soon as they gained it. They were people I connected with through a business networking site. I knew some of their backgrounds based on their profiles and posts. When I came out to them, what started as a positive note quickly turned sour. The first asked for my contact information then quickly set up an "interview" for a podcast they were doing. It caught me off guard, and I quickly contacted them to say I thought we were going to have a chat as I was not prepared to be so publicly transparent about myself. They gave a polite "OK" and then proceeded to ignore me. The second person was someone local who had a penchant for playing "Devil's Advocate" in conversations. If I said I liked something, they immediately took an opposite viewpoint to try and change my mind. I quickly closed myself off to them and said very little during the rest of the conversation. They said how much they enjoyed trying to change people's opinions, as it was like a game to them. I don't appreciate that type of person as it creates an unsafe atmosphere for me. I quickly disconnected from both individuals, knowing it was better to disassociate than risk giving them another chance to affect my personal wellbeing.

So, who can I trust?

The answer became very clear to me. I had a wife and daughters I could trust. For what felt like the first time in my life, I had friends I could trust. Through transition, I learned to trust again because there were people out there—other women—who entered my life and showed me I could trust them, and they had my back.

There will be people in life who will prove untrustworthy for various reasons. Their actions and betrayals can devastate our ability to trust anyone else again. Yet if we keep our eyes open instead of dropping them to the ground, if we continue to believe there are others out there who truly care about us, then those trustworthy people magically appear in our lives at the moments when we most need them. Each one of those loving people are worth more in our lives than everyone who hurt us in the past, combined.

38

Reconnections and Positive Interactions of September and October

Beyond the pain I dealt with at the end of August, I had a sense of independence blossoming inside, a cautious freedom. I made the decision to get off the fence between the façade I wore for so many years, my "male representative," as one person would call it, to move into the everyday light as the woman I was who'd been hidden deep inside. I was starting over, finding my way, beginning with a few new connections made over the previous months. With each new contact, I had to determine how deep I could safely go in talking about my experience without outing myself in the process.

I knew I wasn't ready to broadcast my transition to the world. It's not that I couldn't tell everyone, as broadcasting such news would be easy to do with some type of post or email message. I was still concerned about how people might react to such a public announcement. I've seen too many negative news articles and social-media posts, and the thought that I could become a target and possibly find my life in danger made it difficult. I was an introvert who learned the painful lessons taught by her father… I had to stay silent to stay safe. I never spoke with my family beyond the most superficial level. When I was transparent about myself, their response was swift and negative: spankings, teasing, and ridicule.

I rarely interacted with other people in work or social settings. Identifying as someone I wasn't, made it all the harder to have real conversations with anyone. Superficial conversations allowed me to sink into the background and not be noticed, as I feared someone could recognize the real me. Thus, even in public situations, to stay silent was to stay safe.

Yet I was beginning to blossom, to be who I was created to be. While Jordan was the first person from the past I contacted, he wasn't the last. His openness and friendship allowed me to take the baby steps of reconnecting with more people over the next month.

I thought about people in my past who I liked, women with whom I thought I could connect, and let know about my transition. Three ladies quickly came to mind. I contacted Blaire and Mary Ann to learn more about the organizations for which they worked. Both firms were similar to a place I worked before, where I'd first met all three of them. Within my initial message, I asked about their companies and alluded to having made personal changes and wanting to connect with their company HR departments. After their positive responses at reconnecting and letting me know about their organizations, I came out to each of them. As with Jordan, their responses were filled with positive energy. I felt safe talking with them, and soon we had video chats set up to reacquaint ourselves, rekindling friendships anew from where we left off so long ago. Like Jordan, each one said she wanted to remain with me on this journey, to stay connected and see how, and where, our friendships would grow.

While it was only a handful of relations from my past, each person was so positive talking with me, in their openness of wanting to stay connected, it was like a healing salve, especially after the sour conversations with family members over the summer. Their support laid the groundwork for me to open up to more people.

My focus was on HR. They were supposed to be the most supportive part of an organization and would be a good place for me to be up-front about being a trans woman. The responses were mixed, though no one was overtly negative.

The third lady was someone I rarely interacted with in the previous organization, yet there was something about her that felt safe to me. As with the other ladies, I took a step of faith, and the result was just as amazing. Like the others, we reconnected and began to develop a friendship. It was nice to learn about her and what was going on in life and to just share thoughts as friends. With all three women, I felt safer talking and being open with them than I ever had before my transition.

Besides reconnecting and growing friendships during those months, I was feeling more confident in public. Sure, going to the mall where people knew me was always a safe bet, and it was getting easier to meet with the people from my past. Yet, there were times I still had to enter sites where my old, legal name was required, such as medical facilities.

During those two months, I had visits for scheduled appointments and unexpected visits with a new medical provider. When I set up my first appointment, I mentioned having a preferred name; she used that name for me during the rest of our conversation, making sure to enter it in their medical records. Even knowing my preferred name was in the system, I still felt nervous checking in with my identification showing my male name. I was just coming out into the world full time. It meant every interaction had the opportunity to either boost my confidence or suppress it. I hoped for the best... and was never disappointed. I was always addressed by my preferred name. I was treated with respect during each visit, including one visit to the ER. No one questioned me. No one said anything that might create an embarrassing or painful experience.

During those two months there were ample opportunities to meet people for the first time as Susannah. I was careful to see how they would react to me once they knew the truth. With every conversation, with every visit where I showed my identification, I was taking steps of faith, and the Lord showed me people who were kind, caring, and wanted to know the real me, Susannah. Thus, in November, I would begin taking bigger strides of faith and pray the Lord would walk with me, guide me with every step... And He did.

39

The November Miracles

Although it began innocently enough, November became one of those amazing months where prayers were answered in miraculous fashion. The last two weeks of the month were filled with unforeseeable joy. I dreamed—prayed—such things would happen, yet never expected the outcomes nor the speed with which they occurred. I was over fifty, too old, I thought, for such opportunities to happen.

To set the context, it was a Sunday in the middle of the month when I prayed that the following week would include one miracle per day. It was a very simple prayer with no stipulations for what I hoped would occur, no expected outcomes. My faith only asked for what The Lord wanted for me. I went to bed not knowing what would happen, falling asleep believing wonderful things would occur over the next few days.

On Monday, around noon, I received a simple email. After reading it, I began jumping around my home thanking the Lord: I was selected to be featured in Sephora's "We Belong" video series, and one of my friends from the store, Kendra, would be in the video with me. It was the video series a district director had been asking me to apply for since February, and I finally sent in my application in mid-October. A store director was asked to guide me through the process, as she was featured in the same video series earlier in the year. She told me after my application went in to not expect anything too soon as they took almost a year to select her story. Yet there was the message saying my story was not only selected, but they also wanted to film in three weeks and post it on Instagram at the end of December.

I quickly sent notes off to friends and supportive family members about the email. They were also excited by the news, and enthusiastically asked when the filming would occur. While I thought I was excited, Kendra was thrilled since we would be in the video together.

The next day, when visiting my Sephora store, I was amazed by the enthusiasm of the beauty advisors I spoke with about the video. I returned home and sent a message to my wife suggesting it may be time to legally change my name. It was a topic we discussed on and off for a couple months, though hadn't made a decision. Her response was a positive emoji showing three thumbs up.

Tuesday night I completed the paperwork to file for my legal changes. Wednesday morning, I went into the county courthouse to file my petitions. While in line, I heard the probate officer telling others it was taking up to six weeks to receive the signed judgments, though a few had mailed out within a couple weeks. It was nice to have an idea of when to expect my documents. Now that the petition filings were happening, it was my sincere hope to have my signed and certified copies by Christmas.

The first three days after my prayer were amazing; on the fourth day was my third-ever hairstyling appointment. It was a blessing of its own to sit in the chair as Maeve worked her magic with my hair. The timing felt perfect, with the filming scheduled to take place in three weeks. During the three-hour appointment, we talked about care and styling of my hair as she trimmed and highlighted it. When she was done, my hair was lighter than after the previous appointments, and she gave me some tips for how to dry and style it for the big day. Every visit with Maeve was like a new haircare lesson for me. She was always so genuine to talk with, answering my questions and giving me new tips to improve my haircare. Every visit felt like a magical event, with me leaving her salon with hair more beautiful than I could imagine.

Friday was a wonderful end to the week. I had a half-hour conversation with my Sephora producer. She provided details on what would happen the day of filming. Kendra and I were to start at the Sephora store for about an hour of filming before going to a separate site for the interview and additional filming. During our chat, my producer asked for more information regarding my background, to talk about things not included in the brief write-up I'd provided in my original application. That was when she learned about my love of storytelling and how I was writing a memoir of my transition, and how important the beauty advisors at Sephora were to making my journey so successful.

It was an amazing week with so many miracles, yet Saturday provided the biggest marvel of the week—of the year, to be honest. When I opened the mailbox, inside were two self-addressed envelopes I had written at the courthouse only four days prior. I was so close to skipping all the way to my house, both anxious and nervous at what might be inside. The probate officer told people it would be two-to-six weeks to receive the judgments, so did this mean something was wrong? Or was this going to be a miracle to top all the previous ones combined? In the house, I quickly opened the envelopes to find my legal judgments in them. Within four days of filing for the biggest change of my life, my dreams of a half century had come true with legal changes that included my name.

I bounced around the house in the excitement of the moment. While I kept my last name, the names my dad gave me were no longer valid. Relief washed over me to be free of names I disliked. Instead, my first and middle names were replaced by words that truly identified me for who I was, and always knew I'd been. The clunky identifiers of the past were now replaced by the elegance of my true nature. Reading those judgments was like the removal of a heavy burden, the removal of deadweight that held me back all my life.

With the name change completed, the next ten days brought the two steps preordained by the judgments: I needed to update my social security and change my driver's license. Many offices were closed or had limited appointments due to the pandemic. Thus, I knew calling social security could take a few days. However, they set me up with an in-person appointment that very afternoon. One down, one to go.

The department of motor vehicles (DMV) was a bit trickier. The online scheduling system said nothing was available near me for six weeks, putting it after the new year began. I wasn't about to let such news hold me up, so I searched for any location with an appointment in the current calendar year. I found an office with an opening the next afternoon. All it required was a forty-minute drive, which was nothing to me if it meant I could get my new driver's license and update my registration right away. The next day I entered the DMV office, a bit nervous as I was about to change my personal identification with the state. Within twenty minutes, I left having updated my license and registration. Even more amazing was seeing a photo I actually liked on my license. My first stop after leaving the DMV was my Sephora store to show my new license to whichever friends were there. Stopping there was my way of going straight to my family, to the people I knew cared about me. Their excitement for me was full of love. No one cared if my card was the temporary license, instead celebrating the fact it was legal proof of who I really was, of my true identity in this life.

In between those two appointments was Thanksgiving. It was a day for which I had much to be thankful for, to thank the Lord for the blessings He bestowed on me. My name now reflected who I've always been, and it meant so much to see the legal proof confirming what I always knew, what I prayed for since those early years.

November brought so many wonderous events, yet there was by no means a reduction of miracles to come. December brought its own magic, its own creativity and special times, which combined to bring the year to an amazing and enchanted close.

40

December Magic

The amazing events of November were a precursor to the magical month of December. December was a busy month, with more tasks to complete than any month for quite some time.

Now that my legal changes were certified, I had a laundry list of items and places to update. I prioritized which items to update right away, and which could wait until after the first of the year. I had significantly more items to update due to my age. Besides financial institutions and various insurance policies, there were utilities, memberships, accreditations, restaurant apps, university records, and Veterans Affairs records to update.

I had to decide how to approach my online profiles like Facebook, Instagram, and LinkedIn. Did I want to start over, or just change the existing profile names and see what happened? The latter would be outing myself, whether actively or passively. There were so many other things on my plate heading into the end of the year, I decided to leave those decision for the new year.

The first week included many of the more important updates, plus previously scheduled meetings. The first meeting was to see Blaire in person for the first time since 2013. The Zoom call with her was great, yet seeing her in person, face-to-face, was an amazing way to start the month, especially since I saw very few people in the real world except my friends at Sephora and MAC. She was in the first handful of people from my past who I saw in person after my transition. I was nervous about my appearance even though we had the video chat in September. I was so happy to see her, and she was as amazing as I could have hoped when we talked. When it was time to go, she gave me a hug and talked about making sure to get together again.

I brought her some of the Christmas sugar cookies I made right before Thanksgiving. It was a much-loved tradition for me, making those cookies with my gramma's recipe, and a batch of fudge. While I usually shared them with family, this year was different, as I had no family nearby with whom to share. Yet I loved making the soft, almost cake-like cookies, which stayed that way for quite a while when they were securely sealed. I brought some for Blaire and her family, along with a copy of my gramma's recipe so she could make them if she wanted. Her excitement at such a simple gift meant even more to me.

I found myself balancing my time between networking calls during the week and doing name updates. The updates, especially those that required a phone call, often took a half hour to an hour to complete, longer if I had to wait for an operator. At the same time, insurance required routing to different departments for auto, home, etc., thereby taking upwards of a couple hours to complete the process.

While name updates were ongoing, the second week shifted my focus to preparing for the Sephora video shoot and interview. I began with a brow wax in Sephora and ended with a manicure the day before filming. In between, I made outfit and makeup decisions since I was responsible for both. After taking photos in different outfits, I stopped by Sephora to see Kendra and others for their thoughts on my options. Kendra and I knew boots were non-negotiable, so if a dress didn't work with boots, it was rejected. Finally, we decided on two outfits. The first was a navy-blue turtleneck-sweater dress that stopped midthigh paired with over-the-knee black boots. The second was a burgundy floral-print dress that stopped above my knees with brown knee-high boots. The second dress included an optional grey duster-length open sweater with a hood. Kendra was thrilled with my choices; her opinions going into the selection process were important since we'd be in the video together and needed to align our outfits to some degree.

It was hard to sleep the night before filming. I was excited and anxious for how it would turn out. I woke up early to get ready for the day's filming, and though I tried to have everything set out the night before. I still made last minute changes to my makeup and outfits.

When I arrived at the store, Carol opened the door. It was great seeing her and having another friendly face alongside Kendra's. After meeting the film and audio team, we spent the next hour shooting several videos of Kendra and me interacting in different parts of the store. Even though we had to remain in masks for filming inside the store, Kendra and I had a lot of fun, talking about makeup and life as we usually did while they told us what types of shots they wanted to take. Most of the time it felt like the two of us were just giggling and relaxed, two girls enjoying the fun of having a makeup store all to ourselves!

After a short drive to the interview site, Kendra and I had a half hour to change outfits. The space Sephora selected was open and nicely furnished with a selection of chairs and sofas. Kendra and I asked the team to take a few photos of us with my camera, without masks. The first photos were in the outfits we wore in the store filming, while the rest were after our wardrobe change for the interview.

I was so glad to have Kendra there with me. She helped me stay relaxed though the entire filming process, both in the store and at the interview site. As we sat on a sofa for the interview, we answered questions while giggling, laughing, and generally having fun. There were a few tear-filled moments, like when I talked about my negative experiences with my dad. When I mentioned how much Kendra's hug meant to me after I told my dad I was trans, she teared up too. I hoped the interview process would be positive; our conversation with the interviewer, who was also our producer, turned out to be even more fun than I expected. During the filming process, Kendra and I found we were more like sisters than we originally realized.

Additionally, I felt safe around the filming team. Both men were kind and personable, creating a positive environment for me. For most of my life, I wasn't totally comfortable around men. However, these two were always smiling, spoke kindly, and created a very affirming space around me. They were even willing to listen to my desire to have them take video of Kendra and me with a "flocked" 6-foot Christmas tree between us, which ended up in the final film version. When the filming was over, part of me wished it would continue, as I enjoyed my time in that setting. I felt naturally myself the entire day.

With filming done, I spent a lot of time over the next days writing, editing, and re-editing one of the most important emails of my life. It was a message to my dad, brothers, and aunt to inform them of my legal name change. There were so many ways I could write it, yet to match my personality and the importance of God in my life, I wanted to craft it to be direct, yet soft with love. It was not an easy task. I let them know I had the full support of my wife and daughters and was blessed to have many Christian women alongside me on this journey. After telling them my new primary email address, I closed with the following statement:

> I expect many will not agree with, nor support, who I am. Please know I love and accept each of you for who you are and where you are at with this—without judgment. Also, I have known my true self—who I have always been—since the age of three. Now that I can be myself wherever I go, I've finally begun to return to the outgoing person I was so long ago in early childhood.

No one responded to my email, which wasn't a surprise. However, the previous weekend I informed my middle brother, the same one I came out to in June, so he knew it was coming in case there was any backlash. When I touched base with him a couple days after my note, he said he'd heard nothing from anyone.

Within days of sending the message to family, my youngest daughter arrived to spend two weeks with me for Christmas. During the first week, when the weather was good, we went to meet friends she made during the summer at Sephora. Then we baked more cookies and watched movies. We made a turkey dinner for Christmas, and with the leftovers I showed her how to make a Holiday Leftover Burrito, which we both enjoyed eating a few times.

The second week the weather turned cold with a touch of snow. It created a beautiful wintery scene outside, and we were able to go for walks and enjoy the quiet of the snowy environment. We spent more time at home, enjoying the holiday scenery in the home, creating new meal ideas with leftovers, and watching movies. On a day when the weather was clear, we managed to see an early movie in a theater, the first I'd seen since the pandemic shut things down. What mattered most, however, was our time together, as my daughter is one of my greatest joys in life.

During the last week of December, the Sephora video with Kendra and me premiered on Instagram. When I received a message that it was posted, I was both excited and nervous. Kendra and I spent over an hour talking and answering various questions during the interview, which meant it was hard to know what would make the final cut and how the story might be laid out.

As I watched the video for the first time, it was almost an out-of-body feeling, a sense of trying to remember speaking the words I saw myself saying in the video. There I was on the small screen talking about my background, how I felt forced to pull away from family and society due to how I was treated when I tried to exhibit being the girl I knew I was. I saw myself talking about the importance of Sephora in my life and seeing Kendra sitting beside me saying how we now see ourselves more as siblings than customer and employee. Then there was the moment when I told the whole world about the venom in my dad's words after I came out to him, and how important Kendra's hug was afterwards.

The video was four minutes long, one of the longest "We Belong" videos I'd seen. The supportive comments posted by viewers and the positive "heart" reactions almost brought me to tears. The posts were overwhelmingly positive, including a couple where the person said my story was so much like their own. Knowing my story touched people in such a positive way felt incredible.

I watched the video with my daughter, who then told me she was proud of me. It wasn't the first time she said that, nor would it be the last. After the first of the new year, it was time for her flight home, and I received a pass to accompany her through security. It was my first time doing so as my true self, with my new ID. Although I was nervous, my ID was checked and there were no problems going through the body scanner. It was a good thing I was with her, as her flight was delayed for a few hours. It gave us more time together, which we both enjoyed. As she gave me a last hug before getting in line to board her flight, she looked up at me and told me again she was proud of me. I held back my tears and gave her another big hug.

I missed her already, watching her walk through the gate door towards her flight. She was a special part of an amazing end to 2021. The most important legal changes were done, the video was public, and I was able to spend time with my youngest daughter.

41

Enter the New Year

January was a month of key changes, updates, and observations. Only four months before, I had actively decided to get off the fence and live as the woman I've always been. Those four months, I slowly found my own stride to move forward. After the small steps to contact a handful of people from my past, came the larger affirming actions, spearheaded by legally changing my name. My old self finally sloughed off, offering a sense of freedom and renewed strength. It was like removing a ball and chain from my neck.

The sense of freedom included a readiness to update my social media sites, beginning with Facebook. The last week of December, I scrubbed my site to remove all aspects and photos of my past. While I was never very active on Facebook, I still wondered if anyone would notice. All my photos were removed, and I untagged myself from photos connected to my site. No one noticed the changes, or at least said anything.

The first week of January, I posted a new header photo showing a trail in the woods, along with my name change. The photo was appropriate, resembling how I now made my own trail, cutting a new path through the forest of life. After a few days, seeing that my number of friends remained the same as before the scrub, I took the biggest step I could think of: I added my new profile picture. I was nervous selecting a photo. Who might notice the change? Would anyone negatively comment on the pho-to? Would my friend list suddenly dwindle? The day of the major up-dates, the response was amazing. There were positive reactions from people I'd never told about my transition, along with some amazing and beautiful comments regarding my photo. My fears were being laid to rest.

The logical follow-up to that success was to merge my old LinkedIn profile with my new one. Though I contacted the first three people I came out to in August through my old site, those initial messages were carefully written as my "old" self. In January, however, I selected a couple-dozen people to message through my old profile to straight-up tell them about my transition and impending profile revision. It took a lot of time to craft each message, even when using a baseline template for each one. Being so open, coming out to people I hadn't really connected with in years, was nerve-rack-ing, as I awaited whatever response they might send… if they even responded.

What happened next was short of a miracle. Apart from three messag-es that never received a response, and a couple questionable replies, such as "trying to understand," everyone was very positive. Those who asked for the Sephora link were amazingly supportive. Some of the most beauti-ful responses came from women I never had close connections with in my past. Yet from our limited interactions, they were women I actually looked up to as possible role models. They were ladies I wanted to talk with and maybe create real friendships with before my transition, yet couldn't be-cause they only knew me for what I identified as, not for who I've always been. One, in particular, became the catalyst for helping me change my university student records.

Three messages went to men whose Christian faith was strong. I spent hours drafting those messages, wanting to remain connected, yet unsure where they would truly stand regarding me being transgender. The first reply was one of the questionable ones, asking some questions while say-ing they were "trying to understand" to be supportive. The other two were more positive, focused on the fact they had known me for many years, they knew my character from our time together, and therefore viewed my "outside" as being just the housing for my soul.

I no longer felt I was alone in the world. For two years, those who knew me best never knew me before my transition. Now, almost three-dozen people from my previous life knew I was a trans woman, and they were onboard and supportive of me taking those steps to live as the woman I'd always known I was. It was heartening to have friends who were aware of my truth.

Even with the positive vibes from friends, not everything in my life was rosy. I was still on an emotional roller coaster. In many ways, being transparent allowed me to let out emotions I had pent up for much of my life. It also meant that buried pains, things from the past I had tried to forget, were churning up to the surface—into the light. I felt something still holding me back. I always knew I could fly higher and farther as a woman than I could while trying to identify as something I wasn't. Yet, I had a sense of pain and panic, a fear I could never be successful. Then, as with every problem before, I took this to the Lord in prayer.

As I prayed, I realized how I often kept myself back, finding reasons to believe I would never be successful. At times, everyone I looked up to for support seemed to look down on me. I began to cry, aware that my dad, one of the most influential people in my young life, never told me he believed I could be successful doing anything I wanted to do. He treated anything I was curious about that didn't interest him as a negative choice. He was adamant success was only possible if I did things that were significant to him. He didn't care that none of his interests remotely fascinated me. I kept hearing him tell me I would fail at everything I was interested in and wanted to do, so success at failing became embedded in me from an early age.

Even as an adult, what I liked never seemed good enough for my dad. He often told me there was no success in a life of writing. Instead, he recommended pursuing something that mattered in this world, suggesting I work for a company where I could prosper. He alluded to my brothers who were very successful in their family lives and careers, implying he viewed me as a failure. I was the black sheep of the family long before coming out.

I considered the pain which held me back, and it was tied to another insight that was just as difficult. Ever since childhood, people have tried to put me in a box to describe what or who I am. Male. Program manager. Budget person. Stoic. Freelance writer in "X" niche. It got to the point where it seemed I had to self-identify in a box, as it was the only way I could have value to other people.

The reality is, I didn't fit a "box" before my transition, and now that I'm starting to fly, I'll never fit a box. Who I am is more than the sum of my experiences, and my abilities far outweigh a simple description or a basic niche identifier. When I see how people will only value me if I put myself in a box and label it for their ease and convenience, I realize how wrong it is for both parties. For me, a box is like a cage. It restricts me to the point of being confined and unable to grow to my true abilities. For them, they miss out on a wealth of opportunities where I can provide new ideas, help view organizations from a new perspective, and write amazing stories that I can only do when I'm outside that box.

While my dad was at the center of these issues, I still chose to move forward and accept how they affected me more than I'd like to admit while refusing to hold any grudge against my dad. He had no idea of the pain he caused, as that was who he was—and still is. For me to heal, I look at what happened, accept how things were done, and remind myself it is now past. Then I forgive. Through my entire transition, forgiveness— refusing to hold a grudge—has been the answer and the path to healing. By letting go of the pain and forgiving those who caused it—whoever they may be—I can accept myself for how I was created, succeed without guilt, and fly higher than I ever dreamed.

42

I'm Not What I Used to Be, Yet I Am Who I've Always Been

For most of my life, it seemed the only option available to me was to identify and live according to the body I grew up in. Although I knew I was a girl inside, family and society did their best to mold me into a boy and then a man. It never felt right. Sure, there was plenty of testosterone flowing through my body, yet it never convinced me I was a man. I knew my real persona was female, shut away from daylight, stuck in the dark closet I'd been trapped in since childhood. While I considered coming out and starting my life as a trans woman many times over the years, just thinking about those first steps was difficult and scary. It hurt to know I was female and still had to keep it hidden from the world, to try to live a life aligned with the shell I was given. In reality, I was living a shell of a life.

There were many times I felt the fierce pain of having to identify as someone I wasn't. Thus, it shouldn't be surprising how often I wished the pain would go away... that I could go away. I didn't want to experience it. If I was gone, then the pain would be gone, and I would no longer be a disappointment to family or a bother to others. If I was gone, they could live their lives in their own perfect worlds, free from having to deal with a trans person in their lives. Yet I was made by God in His image, given life by Him, and provided a strong will to live through whatever adversity befell me. God knew what I didn't: He would answer the prayers of my three-year-old self at a time of His choosing, and that time is now. God put a simple message on my heart: He 1) loves me; 2) has always loved me; and 3) will always love me. This message isn't just for me, either; it's for everyone.

My approach to people was to look at the person, not just the "package." It also aligns with the Bible verse in Samuel where the Lord's focus was on the heart, not the appearance. I'm a woman, yes... a trans woman, whose wish is to be allowed to live my life as the woman I am, the woman I've always been at my spiritual heart.

I expect to lose many acquaintances and family members as I finally come out to them. I'm prepared for that. There were never many friends in my life, and none who showed any interest in wanting to know me or hang out with me. There was no sense of reciprocal caring from them in the fashion I imagined occurred between real friends. Only during the past two years have I begun to meet—and in some cases, reconnect with—people who felt like, and have become, the type of friends I was missing in my life: people who seem to care about and support me the way I care about and want to support them. Over time, they're the ones who felt more like family to me than the ones I grew up with. It's the feeling I have with the associates at my Sephora store who have been with me on this path, especially since Mom's death.

I think of the few hugs I received over the years before transition. I was always a hugger at heart, yet I felt self-conscious hugging. I was never sure what was right or wrong. My understanding was that men don't hug. Since I was viewed as being male, my hugs were supposed to be stiff, more of a "hi" than an emotional connection. Women, however, hug each other frequently. Each hug is a symbol of the connection between them, a bond of friendship. They aren't afraid to let their emotions show. Hugs are a natural extension of who they are as women and friends. That was missing throughout my life—natural friendships, a personal connection with other women. Because it was a part of the real me, it, too, was closed off from the world, relegated to the closet.

Although I could accept hugs, I never initiated them as I had no real understanding of when it was proper. And yet, just six months into my HRT transition, those types of hugs began to flow my way. When one of my new friends came up to me and initiated a hug, I immediately felt accepted, realizing the connection so often experienced between two women. I finally felt I was where I belonged, the woman I've always been.

My transition is personal, and it feels right because I kept my faith in God with every step. I know and affirm Jesus Christ as my savior. The Holy Spirit helped me find a new calm in my life and filled me with peace. I am a child—a daughter—of God. I know God made me the way I am, while putting the wonderful people who accepted and supported me on my path in life, the ones who became so dear to me as I struggled with each step to get here. God never makes mistakes. It's also why I looked to Him as I considered when and how to come out to my family.

The coming-out process was fraught with dilemmas, thinking about which family members to open up and come out to. Because I heard comments during family gatherings, my expectations for them having positive reactions were low. The only family members I opened up to about who I was prior to my transition were those I believed would not berate me, who would continue to love me no matter what I said. Sadly, they've both passed away.

With the rest of my family, I expected the worst, so anything above that would be a plus. In so many ways, I never felt I truly belonged around family. Opening up to them was difficult, yet by the end of my second year of transition, my being a woman was no longer hidden in the shadows. Except for one brother, I haven't spoken in depth with any family member since coming out to them. I guess I placed the bar low enough, as it seems I no longer have the family I grew up with.

When I think about the people in my life who I will lose due to my coming out, including family, God reminds me of the friends I've made since starting my transition. I'm reminded how many of them told me over the months how much my being in the store made their days, how happy they were when I showed up. Some even mentioned looking forward to seeing me on the days they knew I would stop by. Julie and I talked about why it took me a couple of months to finally start asking her questions… I went to talk with her nearly two months after Mom died in 2020. My delay was due to my introverted nature, being shy, and often slow to take the initial steps to open up and reach out to others. It was especially difficult for me to speak with the ladies in Sephora I really wanted to meet, as I felt I needed to have a good reason, the right question, before starting a conversation. Julie told me how, before I initiated talking with her in October, other associates were already talking about me in the breakroom. In September, she said, "Everyone was talking about how great Susannah was so much, that I was saying to myself, 'I want to talk with Susannah, too!' It just took time to connect."

It felt good to be wanted. I often worried I was in people's way, taking up their valuable time. I was often uneasy about being in the store too long when I stopped by. Yet, whenever I mentioned my concern, the beauty advisors just reiterated how glad they were that I was there. Some of them constantly apologized for leaving me to help other customers, yet my response was to always tell them there was no need to apologize. They were working and had customers to assist.

And yet, based on conversations with my friends, I realize how many of the ladies I've known less than two years became the support group I'd longed for most of my life. They were happy to see me, cared about how I was doing, and were willing to share personal information so I could return the sentiment and care for them, too. Though I may not have a similar community anywhere else in my life, that's alright. What I do have now is the community I need, what I've longed for all my life.

While writing these closing thoughts about my friends, I understand something more deeply than before. The women who were with me at the beginning—Christmas 2019—and everyone who joined my journey at various points since my mom's passing…it's clear to me: I never would have made it this far without all of them. Their support kept me going, helped me to expand my boundaries—my comfort zones—while accepting the pace that was most comfortable for me.

It all takes me back to something I believed when I was young: I could do anything as a girl.

Now that I'm older, it still holds true: As a woman, I can do and accomplish anything.

43

Short Story: Hope

Hope

A Short Story by Susannah Dawn

It was seven years since I last walked the neighborhood streets of my youth. My hometown never took kindly to change, which kept things predictably the same. During that period, I changed in a way no one could predict. In high school everyone knew me as Henry, a skinny introvert who kept to himself and was often harassed by the school bully. Every day was a struggle just to stay one step ahead of him and his pack. By the end of college, I transitioned to Hope, a trans woman who found the confidence she had lacked for so much of her life.

On my third night in town, I planned to walk those streets on my own, not knowing another change would occur before the evening was over.

The evening began simply enough. My parents and I went to a local restaurant, Mama's Italiana. As we entered, the aroma of pizza and pasta filled me with fond memories of one of my only high-school friends, Kelli. Her parents owned the restaurant, and Kelli greeted us when we arrived.

"Welcome back!" she said to my parents. "It's great to see you all, though I don't recognize the young lady with you."

"Hi Kelli," I said quietly, watching for her reaction.

Kelli did a doubletake as I felt the gentle touch of my mom's hand on my back, letting me know she was there for me. I glanced at my parents, who were both smiling, before turning back to Kelli.

"Henry?" she said as if trying to see the old me somewhere within my face. "Is it really you?"

"It's me, Kelli, although now my name is Hope."

"Hope," she said softly to herself. I saw her eyes go up as if the name rolled about in her mind. She looked back to me and said, "It's so good to see you! I've got just the table for you all."

Kelli led us to a spot off to the side with few customers. After taking our orders she asked, "Do you mind if I join you? I've got a break coming up, and I'd really love to catch up with you... Hope."

"I'd like that, Kelli," I said. "I really wanted to see you tonight."

After bringing out our entrées, Kelli sat down beside me with an orange Italian soda and side of fries. "So, Hope, tell me everything!" The genuine excitement on her face felt good.

"Dear, you don't have to say anything you're not comfortable telling Kelli in front of us," Mom said. Mom always had a way of saying the right thing, making me feel safe knowing she was looking out for me.

"Let me say something first," Kelli said. I nodded to her. "I've always thought you'd make a wonderful girl."

I blushed.

"It's true, Hope! Although I don't know why I thought that, whenever it crossed my mind, it just made sense to me."

"Thank you," I said, thinking about how to start.

"I guess this story began during the first year of college, with the gal who became my best friend—and big sister—while I was there: Miriam. Though she was a year ahead of me, she was in my first-semester history class. We connected on a small-group term paper, with three of us in the group, including Melody. The two of them really listened when I talked, never judging me or what I said. It felt safe to be open in front of them. As our history topic was focused on women and the expansion of the country, during one of our meetings I was a bit more open and honest than expected. I admitted my admiration of those strong women in the past and said that I had always felt I was a girl, not a boy."

"How long have you known?" asked Kelli. Her questions gave me a chance to fit in bites from the lasagna in front of me. It was one of my favorite dishes.

"I guess all my life," I said. "However, and my parents know this, when I first realized it, I could tell they were not accepting of such ideas. So, I forced myself to bury that part of me."

"I knew it!" said Kelli.

"Let her continue," said Mom, "or she won't be able to finish her story before your break is over." Mom winked at Kelli, who returned it with a big smile.

"When Miriam asked if I still felt that way, I paused to think. I knew that whatever I said might set a critical tone. I also trusted them and decided to be honest in my reply. I admitted to still feeling that way, and about the strong fear inside to say or do anything about it for fear of being bullied, like I was in high school."

"You mean Darius Black," Kelli said.

"Yes, Darius." Although the few bites I had of my lasagna as we talked allowed good memories to flow over me, the name of my bully sent a cold chill down my spine.

"He's still in town, you know," she continued, "as are most of his gang from school. I don't think he'd recognize you now, though. Besides, nowadays he seems more focused on drinking beer and working at the mill."

"Go on, Hope," Dad said in his kindly way. "Continue your story, and let's leave Darius behind."

"Thank you, Papa." After a deep breath I continued.

"It was Melody who was quick to support me that day, telling me how she was bullied in school for liking girls. Though the reasons weren't the same, we had a mutual understanding between us from our experiences."

Noticing my mouth was feeling a bit dry, I took a drink of water before continuing. "It helped to have a shared experience with Melody, although it was Miriam who took me under her wing. The first thing she did was bring me to her church, saying how prayer often helped her through the biggest decisions of her life."

"I remember when we were in church together here," Kelli said. "Why was that any different?"

"It was in college where I first really opened up to God for help," I said. "Once I did that, I turned to prayer whenever a big decision occurred in my life. Prayer was what allowed me to take my first step out of the dorm as myself, with some help from Miriam and Melody, too. I felt calmer and more comfortable than expected that first time walking out the door. After that, every time and everywhere we went, at least one of them stayed beside me."

Then I told Kelli what they said to me that first day out.

"You look great, Kiddo," Miriam said before we left the dorm. "Do you have a name picked out? We obviously can't call you Henry."

"The name *Hope* came to me last night," I replied.

"I like it!" said Melody.

"Alright, Hope," said Miriam, "let's go for a walk."

"The walk ended up being to the nearby mall," I told Kelli. "I didn't expect that we'd actually go that far, yet after entering the mall, it became the moment when my transformation truly began. After Christmas that first year, I became Hope at college. With the help of Miriam and Melody during our first summer together, no one could tell I wasn't born as Hope when my sophomore year started."

"What about your parents?" asked Kelli.

"She told us before her junior year," replied Mom. "To be honest, we were unsure about her being transgender. However, neither of us stopped loving or supporting her."

"They promised to honor my request to keep my secret from neighborhood friends," I said. "It was shortly after college when I completed my transition, yet it still took me these seven years after leaving for school to finally return to visit my parents and my home."

"Wow!" said Kelli. "That's amazing, and I'm so proud of you." Her smile warmed my heart. "Oh... I have to get back to work. Can we get together again while you're in town?"

"Absolutely, Kelli! I'd love to spend some time with you."

As Kelli gave me a hug she said, "Talk soon."

The few days since I arrived home were spent with my parents and close family. I needed some personal time to walk the streets where I grew up without Mom's interjections of local gossip about the people and places we passed. Thus, when we left the restaurant, my parents turned left to go home while I went right.

The people of the neighborhood would surely remember the awkward boy of my past if he strolled the streets. However, on that warm evening, walking in flats and wearing denim shorts and a pale tank top, no one recognized the young lady I had become. Each step caused my sun-kissed brown tresses to swish over my bare shoulders, as thoughts flickered of both the conversation with Kelli and my transition over the past seven years. The sounds and smells of the neighborhood invaded my mind with thoughts of days gone by. Good memories emerged as I smelled the cooking from Wong's noodle shop, Mrs. Sanchez's burrito cart, and the Smith's donut shop. If I had not just left the restaurant, no doubt I would stop by at least one of those shops, remembering how each had such great selections that always tickled my taste buds!

However, the sights of the town eventually replaced my positive thoughts of the food vendors with those of the boy who bullied and tormented my younger self. Darius Black and his pack seemed to make their purpose in life to harass that awkward teenage boy. They knocked me over at every opportunity, both in and out of school, often taking the lunch Mom lovingly packed for me. Though most people knew what Darius was doing, no one helped me. While a few probably believed I would finally stand up to the bully, I was sure most feared reprisals from Darius and his gang should they help anyone he targeted.

Passing a local pub, and lost in many trains of thought, I glanced through the large window. The interior was a dingy yellow, though it was unclear if it was due to the wall colors, the lighting, or the window itself. The noise from the busy atmosphere inside could be heard though the open side windows as my gaze was drawn to a group of men standing around the end of the bar. One of them stood out as the center of attention, most likely their leader. Yet, when our eyes connected, a flood of memories almost overwhelmed me. It was Darius Black. I froze as the evil gleam in his dark eyes watched the woman staring at him from outside the window. When his face betrayed that he found something oddly familiar about her—me, I broke the contact and continued walking.

"C'mon, boys, we've got a bird to catch outside," I heard him yell to his crew. With whoops and hollers they ran like a pack of wolves out of the pub.

Once their howls cut through the street noise, I knew I was in trouble and began to run as fast as I could. *I wish I had sneakers instead of these flats*, I thought. The night sky and streetlights provided little light to evade my pursuers. The evening air pressed in around me as I tried to remember most of the streets and shortcuts.

When I began my transition in college, Miriam advised me to take a self-defense course. It came in handy a couple of times on campus, though there was never more than one adversary at a time. This time, however, I questioned if even my instructor could be successful against Darius Black and his howling goons.

They chased me through the streets like wolves tracking a wounded animal. From the noises they made, it was obvious they constantly split up and regrouped with the intent to get around me to close their trap. Running from them felt like high school all over again; and like those days gone by, I refused to give up, believing this would be the time I finally escaped. Yet just like the past, it was only a matter of time before they surrounded me.

From his yelling, it seemed the trap took longer to close than Darius expected. However, once I turned into a dead-end alley, there was nowhere for me to run. His pace slowed to a saunter as he moved towards me. Darius was bigger than I remembered, and except for the slight beer gut, the added weight seemed to be all muscle. I recognized most of the gang members as well, though a few looked softer now. The pack snarled and jeered as they closed off the alley, my only avenue of escape. My focus returned to Darius.

"Look boys, it's little Henry Wilson. I always knowed he was odd… jus' didn't knowed he were a sissy!" The others erupted in laughter. "Did ya miss me Henry… or is it Henrietta?"

"I recognize him now," said Ron Jenkins walking past Darius to stand by my right. "I heard someone call him Hope." Another guy moved to my left.

"Hope?! That's a silly name. Y'ain't got no hope of getting outta what we're gonna do to you."

I kept silent. With my back against a wall, I surveyed the surrounding pack. It was then I decided they were not wolves. Wolves had a sense of honor and nobility to them. Before me was a pack of hyenas, whose yelps made it hard to clearly hear what Darius said. The fear I felt while staring at him caused my knees to give way as I dropped to the ground. The pain from hitting the pavement was minor compared to the thoughts about the coming attack. Darius was a brute, but what would he do to me now compared to when I was that skinny boy? As I waited for Darius to strike, one thought pushed its way to my consciousness. Then I spoke for the first time.

"Hello, Darius."

I think the stunned silence from the pack was at hearing my female voice for the first time. Then they erupted into more laughter.

Yup, definitely hyenas.

Summoning what courage I could, I said, "Do you know the great commandments?"

"What are you talking about?! I go to church and hear the padre preach every week. What's that got to do with anything?" he said.

"The greatest commandment is to love the Lord your God with all your heart, mind, and soul. Jesus said the second great commandment is to love your neighbor as yourself. If that is a great commandment, then why do you treat me and others this way? Do you not love yourself?" It was not until the words crossed my lips when I realized, for some unknown reason, my fear was abating.

The rage in Darius grew as his face began to glow crimson. "Look you little pansy! I get 'nough from the padre every week. And I ain't about to let you squirm outta your punishment for being so degradin' around here."

Though my knees were weak, there was renewed strength in my voice. "Darius, it is written to judge not, lest ye be judged the same way you judge others. If you can't do that, then I'll pray for you."

"Henry, I'm gonna pummel ya!"

As Darius closed in to strike, I remembered the Armor of God. The thought of putting the shield of faith up between us came as my left arm automatically rose to block his blow. He struck hard, almost breaking his hand on the object that appeared on my arm: a shield. When he pulled back, the shield disappeared. He struck again, and again the shield returned to block his blow.

"It's the shield of faith," I said in quiet amazement, more to myself.

"What trickery is this?" Darius was livid. He picked up a pipe and struck again. As he did, Ron kicked at my ribs from the side. The shield appeared, and so did a breastplate.

"The breastplate of righteousness!" I was astonished at what was happening. The blows from both men bounced harmlessly away.

"This is impossible," said Darius. "What kind of trick are you playing?"

Strength flowed through my body as I rose to my feet. Looking Darius in the eyes I said, "No trick, Darius. It's the Armor of God." My eyes focused on him while I sensed the others fan out around us. "Are you not familiar with the Armor of God, Darius?"

He looked stunned at my question before steeling his resolve to pummel me.

"The belt of truth. The shoes of the gospel. The breastplate of righteousness. The shield of faith. The helmet of salvation."

As I spoke the name of each piece, it appeared on my body.

While the others began to back away, Darius pulled a knife. He pointed it at me saying, "You got nothin' to fight back with, you freak." As he stepped closer, a glowing white sword appeared in my right hand.

"The sword of the word of the spirit, Darius."

Though Darius kept his knife out front, ready to strike, he froze. Silence fell around us as though the neighborhood itself held its collective breath, waiting for what would happen next.

Looking into his eyes, I broke the silence.

"I forgive you, Darius."

Darius looked at me, his face, his emotions, in turmoil. I was the prey he bullied the most during school. Not only had I stood up to him, I forgave him for what he did to me during all those years of torment. His arms fell to his sides as the knife dropped to the ground. The collective breath of the neighborhood exhaled before the normal evening sounds resumed.

I walked towards Darius. Though the armor disappeared, he remained frozen where he stood, watching me.

"What's my name, Darius?"

Standing within the reach of his arm, I looked up at his face. As my eyes bored through his, his eyes grew wide. Though my words were soft, everyone heard me.

"What's my name, Darius?"

"H...Hope," he replied.

"That's right, Darius. Don't forget it."

The rest of his gang stepped aside to create an unbarred path for me down the alley to the main street. As I walked past my bully, my own personal demon, I felt true calm and a sense of peace. I continued unhindered down the alley.

Long had I been tormented by Darius Black. It was part of the reason it took me so long to come home to see my parents. The demons of those memories haunted my dreams over the years, causing a deep pain I thought would never depart. Yet that night, with four simple words of forgiveness, all the pain from those memories seeped away. On that night, I finally put my past to rest, facing a demon with only my faith. Once on the main street, the air was cleaner, fresher, while the walk home was freer than at any other time I could remember in my life. The past was done, leaving my future open like the blue sky on a bright summer day. From that moment, I could live each day in the present, not having to look back on my past with fear. Now, every day was fresh, filled with renewed hope.

END